Shahrukh Husain, born and brought up in Pakistan, has studied myth and folklore from around the world for many years. She is the editor of *The Virago Book of Witches*, author of *Women Who Wear the Breeches* and *Temptresses: The Virago Book of Evil Women*, several children's books and a play for children. She also writes screenplays. A practising psychotherapist, she is married with two children and lives in London.

Also by Shahrukh Husain

The Virago Book of Witches
Women Who Wear the Breeches
Temptresses: The Virago Book of Evil Women

THE VIRAGO BOOK OF

Erotic
Myths and Legends

SHAHRUKH HUSAIN

CHARTWELL
BOOKS, INC.

This hardback edition published in 2006 by
CHARTWELL BOOKS, INC.
A division of BOOK SALES, INC.
114 Northfield Avenue
Edison, New Jersey 08837, USA

A Virago Book

First Published in paperback by Virago Press in 2002

A CIP catalogue record for this book
is available from the British Library.

ISBN-13: 978-0-7858-2087-1
ISBN-10: 0-7858-2087-6

Typeset in Cochin by M Rules
Printed and bound in Spain by
Rodesa Rotativas De Estella, S.A

Virago
An imprint of
Time Warner Books UK
Brettenham House
Lancaster Place
London WC2E 7EN

For Nick and Mary Wilson with much love.
I hope this proves an enduring and enjoyable
birthday present

I want to thank Aamer Hussein and Ananda Devi
for agreeing without hesitation to write something
for this book despite demanding schedules. Lennie
Goodings for prodding me and the manuscript into
coherence and Elise Dillsworth for her endless
patience and rigour in dotting the i's and crossing
the t's. Also, Harry Robin, in the next world, for
his enthusiasm. I am sorry he is not here
to see the published work.

Contents

Introduction

When my daughter first discovered that I was writing and collecting erotic stories, she dubbed this 'Mum's Perverted Book'. My son, laconic as usual, simply said, 'It's a wind-up. You don't even like porn.'

I'm glad to say that virtually all others who heard about this book were thrillingly keen. This is hardly surprising, since love is as essential to us as breathing, and sexual fulfilment as vital to our sustenance and well-being as food. Yet a taboo came into being at some stage, unannounced and unexplained, which reduced this indispensable and intense energy to a vice. Sadly, its miasma lingers on. Writings from ancient times, though, give us an insight into an entirely different attitude.

Nowhere is the importance of sex in the living of life more evident than in ancient myth and legend where it is the bedrock of events beyond the ordinary. Such accounts encapsulate the theme at the core of this collection: that the sexual encounter is to be both valued and enjoyed. Before recorded history, promiscuity was an important function of the gods. It peopled the world and in turn their fruitfulness enhanced the fertility of the earth. The orgies held by fertility cults on feast days around spring and harvest were sacred ceremonies during which matrons as well as virgins were released from sexual taboo to dedicate their reproductive function to the fertility gods in return for personal and collective blessings. Fertility deities included the likes of Zeus and Aphrodite (Greek), Daghda and Brigit (Irish) and the notorious Ashera/Ashtoreth of the Near East, condemned by the bible among many other scriptures. The renowned abandon of these occasions came from the religious fervour that can be found in many mystical and gnostic works.

This suggests to me that there is more to sexual energy than simply physical gratification – ardour, a frisson and an attitude of sharing and achieving comparable perhaps to dancing where body, mind and emotion are all engaged. Eroticism, then, is holistic: it involves body, emotion and soul, unlike pornography which is body-specific and focuses on the genitalia and the body zones that titillate them.

Everywhere in narratives of the ancient and medieval worlds, we encounter significant, even profound, sexual event. It is underpinned by conflict, anger, desire and humour. It is not finite; it has an influence on the lives of the participants. Its pleasures do not need validation. Sexual sophistication is highly prized for delectation and for worship. It embraces the secular and the divine. These thoughts influenced my choice of sections.

I was aware of a number of sources for this material when I first suggested the idea of this book to Lennie Goodings as my fourth for Virago. So I was not prepared for the disappointment in store. The erotological texts were dry and ponderous, often ludicrous. Also, they were not stories so much as theses, manuals or short examples. I scoured and rejected reams of material because it was too dull, too evasive, too arcane, badly written or poorly translated.

Thankfully, I managed in the end to locate a number of appropriate pre-published works. In addition I was privileged to have contributions especially for this collection, from two outstanding writers. 'The City of Longing' (p. 7) by Aamer Hussein opens 'Awakenings', and 'Powder Figures' by Ananda Devi (p. 229) appears at the beginning of Love Beyond Life (or The Rapturous Gaze). My own contributions fall into two categories: the first group consists of the editing or reinterpreting of work already in translation and the second of straightforward retellings.

I hope that there is something here to appeal to all tastes – and that this work provides both legitimate pleasure and the frisson of daring to attempt the forbidden.

Shahrukh Husain
Queens Park
London

Awakenings

The City of Longing

When I asked Aamer Hussein for a contribution he improvised on Nizami's celebrated Persian text. I'm grateful to him for reviving a faded memory and for an alluring piece of writing.

You have come now to the city of men who wear black: you will want to know why our garb is so sombre. This is the city where night never falls. But there is often a scarcity of light, when lowering clouds loom above us for days and no rain comes. A city of endless gloomy day. But we have time. Sit down here, on the wall. Smoke a pipe with us, and drink a glass of tea. A desert wind blows around us. Soon it will touch your cheek with the ice of Siberia. But we have time. The coals in the brazier are glowing. Sit down and we will tell you our tale. You may decide to follow the path we took. Or you may take our words as warning: ours is not the path of the fainthearted.

So listen: When you leave the city's northern gate, you will come to a rocky hill, hard to climb. Take off your shoes at the foot of this hill. Ascend. Reach its peak.

There you will find a pavilion of stone, formed like a basket. It rests on one rock, suspended from four woven chains. Observe these chains with care: they, too, are carved of stone. Look up, towards the sky. If your eyesight is good you will see, far, far up amid the clouds, the hovering wings of a great bronze eagle.

Your feet will be sore. Bloody, perhaps. You may want to turn back but you'll need to rest. Because there is no other place, you will enter, by climbing over its woven wall, the pavilion, which is large enough for one man only. You will feel a sudden tremor, and the basket, straw-light now, will rise in the air. Buffeted by wind and rain, you will rise till the vessel that carries you comes to rest on a dark cloud. You will feel it shatter around you, shards falling about you in showers.

Then the great bronze eagle, free now from its burden, will swoop down on you to take you in its beak. You will feel the flames of its eyes on your face, you will smell its carrion breath. You might faint.

Have you, our fine young friend, a head for heights?

Sleep if you can. The journey is long, the journey is short.

You will wake to find yourself, naked and sweating in your shreds, on a narrow islet swimming on a wide silver river. No bird, no basket here. You will want to look for leaves to cover your shame, but isn't it better to rinse your sore body in the warm currents of water instead, wash off the weariness of your journey through the clouds?

Enter the river. Close your eyes.

You will open them to see around you a bevy of tender women, their hair and eyes of every colour, their hands soft like the satins of China. They will rub your limbs with water fragrant as the oils of Arabia. The tiny lashes of their fingers will play on your skin till your weariness fades. You will want to touch them, to hold them, to taste them, but they will laugh and push you away, push your face into the water, and then begin their games again when you, spluttering, raise your head.

Then they will weave their bodies into a boat and carry you on their backs to the far banks of the river. On its shores they will dress you in a tunic and trousers of the finest muslin. Follow them. Through groves of trees with leaves of green silk, past gardens of flowers carved from glass and jewels. Even the scent of fruit is of amber and musk. But you will not notice this. Not yet.

This is the domain of Turktaz the Beautiful.

Her slavewomen will lead you to Turktaz's bower.

She reclines in a crystal arbour, on a couch of gold draped in brocades.

Her hair is black and her eyes have lights in their darkness like pieces of jade. Her skin is the colour of sunlight cooled in crystal cups of pale wine.

Sit beside me, she will say, in words that echo the dulcimer's notes. Her arms, like jasmine creepers, will enclose you in fragrance. Her limbs are revealed to your gaze by the white gauze of her garments: her flesh gleams through mere veils, held in place by a broad belt of gem-encrusted platinum.

Recline beside her on her brocade couch.

Cupbearers come and go with jewelled decanters of fragrant wine. Her hands will lift jade cups of liquor to your lips. You will taste jasmine and rose and magnolia. Bitter mingling with sweet. Sip gently of these flavours. Keep a hold on your senses. Raise your eyes to her face. Her lips are waiting, open. Kiss her mouth. Taste the rose and the jasmine, the bitter and the sweet. Then look at her breasts, which the fluttering of her hands has half revealed, so you can see their golden globes. Trail your fingers in the valley between. Her hands will play on your chest, on your belly. Now your hands will descend to her belly. You feel the hardness of platinum beneath your fingers. Her loins are encased by the platinum. You search for the buckle of her belt. You fumble with the drawstring of your trousers. Her kisses distract you. Your body is in pieces: your head lost in the joy of her, your thighs gripped by heat and lassitude, your hands, come to life like birds freed from cages, searching, searching.

Her hands will restrain you. Not now, she says. Kiss me all you want. Touch me, smell me, taste me. But don't knock, don't enter. Wait for my body till the seventh night. You'll find the key, then.

Cupbearers come and go with decanters of wine.

She will push you back into a pile of scented cushions. The strange wines have assaulted the workings of your mind. She rises. You tug at her skirt. She laughs. You watch her go.

Cupbearers, their hands empty now, will take her place on the brocade couch. Seven women, each dressed in one colour of the rainbow. They will tickle you and scratch and bite. Their nails at your nipples, their teeth at your thighs. Your hands, made desperate in their urgency and task, will try to pull one of them to you, to complete the unfinished journey you began with Turktaz the Beautiful. But your lassitude makes you their victim They have their will of you. The hands of one at the drawstring of your trousers, the lips of one taste your mouth, another makes sport with your abject manhood, which, in its unwilling sleep, can still feel the stirrings of a hidden pleasure.

Five nights of this.

Each night you will come to her consumed by the excesses of the night before. Each night her fragrance will revive you. The wine of Turktaz, of her lips, her breasts, her heavy thighs which open a little more, night by night, to your dark and tender probing. Then her laugh and her refusal and her parting back as you, in your drunkenness, lie against the scented cushions and wait for the rainbow women's ministrations.

You will no longer know which passage of joy you have entered or who brings you relief and satiation. You feel your own inner passages invaded by fingers, by tongues, by toys. You can no longer tell when which rainbow-coloured woman has made love to you tonight. Each one the shadow-sister of Turktaz. Your closed eyes will see only the features of Turktaz the Beautiful. On the blank screens of your inner lids, the black letters of her name separate and intertwine.

Te, re, kaf, te, aliph, ze.

The vowel curving upward in fifth position reflects your longing.

Then, only one more waiting night.

You think you know now what to do. You cannot bear another night of this. You will long for the smell of flowers, the taste of fruit, the sight of a leaf falling, dancing on the wind. You will long for the roughness of beer, the sour smell of yoghurt, the soft taste of milk.

You will long for the feeling of flesh on flesh and even more for the joy of flesh enclosed in flesh.

You will long to make Turktaz your possession.

Go again to Turktaz on the sixth night. Recline beside her on her brocade couch. Taste on her lips the jasmine and the rose, the bitter and the sweet. Taste with your tongue the honey trail in the valley between her breasts. Then let your tongue follow the honey trail to her navel. Stroke the heavy velvet of her calves, move upward to the curves of her thighs.

Pour away the wine. Pour it on the satin grass. Spit it into her mouth. But don't let it get to your head.

Cupbearers come and go. You must force her to drink the wine they bring. Turn her wrist, twist her jade cup to her lips. You must say: Give me all tonight, Turktaz. Take all of me. I'm your minion, your slave, your possession. Repay my nights of waiting. I'm sick of sporting with your shadow.

She will push you away. You must insist.

One more night, she says: and then I'm yours.

You have now regained your male strength, your senses. You're prepared to wrestle, to conquer.

You bite her lips.

Your hands assail her breasts.

You rip off her veils.

She will not move.

She has only the protection of her platinum loincloth.

From her right hip hangs the silver key.

Wrest it from its diamond hold. Our strength is in your wrist, in your grasp, the strength of the men in black.

Its lock is between her thighs.

Place the key in its diamond mouth.
Turn.
Taste bliss.
Then fall.

Fall through air, cloud, rain. Sleep if you can: the journey is long, the journey is short. Wake on an islet in the river, half-naked in shredded muslin. Wait for the great bronze bird to take you in its beak, feel the flames of its eyes, smell its furnace breath. Come to the stony cloud and rest a moment, while the splintered stones gather. Watch them weave themselves into a basket. Step into your vehicle. The eagle drops chains from its beak. Fasten them to the basket before they freeze into stone. Now prepare for your journey.

We are at the gates of the city, awaiting you with newly-woven robes of black. You will not wear them? Did you turn away from the hill, or climb to its peak and tumble down? Or were you one of the chosen who didn't see the basket? Did you wait, perhaps, for the bird to come; did you wait in vain? You were away seven nights. Don't you know the secret? The journey takes place while we tell you our story. The choice is yours: turn back from the hill, or fly to the realm of Turktaz. If you return without seeing her, yours is the road of ordinary men; go back to your cities and your wives, to your chores of earning bread and sweating for milk or beer to moisten the bread.

But if you saw her and tasted her wine, learn the secret of the men in black. The first night with Turktaz and her women is the second, and the second is the fifth, and the sixth night is the first again. No one reaches the seventh night. But in six nights you have learned to live with desire. Your forehead is branded with the name of Turktaz, the letters of desire. Venture back to the world of contentment and live forever as the outcast you've become. Or go back to the rocky hill and wait in vain for the basket and the bird. Or live with us, and wrap yourself in black: it reminds you of the emptiness of longing. Stay with us in our city, where night always rests on the brim of day.

A Pastoral Song

Though married, Radha was not awakened until she experienced the 'love-gaze' of Govinda. The seething desire in the original verses fuelled my own adolescent expectations.

Priya the milkmaid shifted the pot of milk from her right hip, straightened her back and tried to hoist it to her head. Radha made no attempt to help her: she watched Priya, her eyebrows raised. They were approaching Vrindavan, the lush woods where Govinda, the dark-skinned cowherd, revelled with the milkmaids of nearby villages. They called him by many names in these parts: the Mountain-wielder, for that time he'd routed Indra, the sky-god, by lifting a mountain on his shoulder; Mohan, for his sweetness and beauty; Manmohan, the Heart-winner, for his beguiling ways. Ah, yes, and the Flute-bearer. But Radha preferred to call him Govinda. The cowherd. It levelled him with other men.

'Help me, Radha.' Priya widened her eyes.

Radha ignored her, and continued to walk, her hips swaying with the weight of her pot and her unspoken disapproval.

'Radha!'

Radha whirled round.

'My back hurts with the weight of the jar.' Priya patted the pitcher at her hip.

'Or the weight of lust,' Radha retorted. In a few moments they would enter the forest and walk past Govinda, sur-rounded by his lovers, singing, playing, dancing and teasing, each trying to be the most alluring, to win the longest kiss, the closest embrace.

'Lust?' Priya exclaimed, pretending to be offended.

'You are no different from the others,' Radha said, and placed her milk carefully on the side of the path. 'They are all under his spell.'

She put her palms firmly under the base of Priya's copper pitcher and pushed upwards. The lid clanked, but not a drop of milk was lost and it was settled on Priya's head. Radha stepped back, watched Priya's arms stretch up languidly to steady and secure the pot, coaxing her bodice to outline her breasts.

'Ardha-chandra,' Radha murmured, as the rounded golden mounds were exposed like half moons gleaming through dark cloud. What was Govinda's irresistible appeal? He was beautiful, indeed, with his curling jet locks and his shimmering skin. But he was spoiled too! The beloved child of Yashodha, who had always had his way with everyone. And how ruthlessly he loved and left the milkmaids! His kisses were scattered among them like drops from the spring showers of Vrindavan.

'He is heartless, Priya. You know how he enchants girls with his music and his smile, and he never knows them again. To him we are all the same.'

Priya's hand flew to her mouth. 'Radha! How can you say such things? He's – he's a god.'

Radha turned away abruptly. 'A god! What god?'

'You may say that,' Priya said slyly, 'because you have a lord of your own.'

Radha preened. 'Ayana-ghosh is a good man.' She smiled. 'He cares for me well.'

'But don't you wonder why we all flock to Govinda?'

'No!' Radha retorted. 'If I were a virgin, I'd shun him. He'd love me and leave me, too, besmirched and poisonous to all men ever after.'

Radha walked on, taking long, fast strides. She could feel the milk swilling from side to side in the pot. Ayana-ghosh's mother and sisters would be waiting for her.

The laughing voices grew louder, and Radha could hear snatches of song from the glade where Govinda's admirers – the laughing, shameless women who were her friends – transformed so astonishingly in the cowherd's presence. Where was their modesty?

'Just glance at him as we pass,' Priya begged. 'Just once. You'll see what we see.'

'Never,' Radha replied. 'My veil stays over my eyes. I look down when I pass a man who is not my husband.'

Suddenly the sounds of laughter from the woods died. The breeze dropped, the trees grew still and the birds ceased fluttering as they dropped to leafy perches. At the same instant, a thrilling sound showered down through the trees. A musical note.

PA: the fifth note of the scale. The erotic note. The note that echoed the lovers' cry of ecstasy. Then a stream of melody. Govinda was playing his flute. Without knowing it, Radha slowed, her body flowing with the current of the tune. Head bent she continued walking, the music swirling in her mind and her body. Govinda's flute grew louder. It was like a flood rising within Radha and she could feel herself being washed away. Then suddenly, mid-flow, it ceased. Radha stopped, her head raised. A slender, dark figure filled her eye, leaning lazily against a tree, his flute held to his lips, his tapered fingers lying still on its polished surface. His eyes were directed into hers, as if he was challenging the reflected image of himself. 'I am yours,' they seemed to say. 'Claim me if you have courage.'

'And I am yours,' Radha's eyes seemed to reply. Her pot slipped and fell. The milk formed a thick pool before it was lapped up by the earth.

With a cry of despair Radha fell to her knees. 'What will I tell my mother-in-law?'

'What does it matter?' Govinda's voice drifted over the heads of the maidens around him. 'Tell her Govinda the cowherd stole it.'

'Who would believe that a cowherd stole milk from a milkmaid?'

Govinda smiled slowly. He was standing over her now, offering her his hand. His fingers were silk against hers as he raised her up and pointed to the scores of copper pots gleaming in rows under the trees. 'Take what you need,' he said.

Radha bowed her head and did as he bade. She poured the milk into her own pot, then folded her hands in thanks. Her gaze was still lowered as she turned to go. But Govinda reached out and placed a finger under her chin, raising her face gently until she was drowning again in the obsidian mirrors of his eyes. 'Oh fair one, if you had gone home and said, "Govinda took my milk, I gave it to him," ecstasy would have been yours.'

Radha tore her gaze from his. She felt his reproach keenly but her self-reproach was greater. Word would get round that she had been with Govinda, that she had let him touch her. Her name would be tarnished. But even as she walked away, Govinda's gaze held her averted eye captive.

'You're late today, Radhika,' her sister-in-law said. 'Where did you stray?'

'Stray?' Radha's heart stopped.

Her sister-in-law's laugh tinkled. 'Dallying with him, were you?'

Radha's blood drained from her face. 'Dallying? With who?'

The girl noticed nothing. 'With my brother, of course.'

Radha's mother-in-law had come in and was standing by the door. Radha dropped her gaze, pulled her veil over her eyes. 'It's a long way and I was tired. The pot was heavy.'

'Did you not take the path through the forest?' the old woman asked.

'Through Madhuban . . . yes . . .'

'So it's Madhuban now, is it? Why are you using the lover's name for Vrindavan?'

'Why, Ma, it is what everyone calls it.'

'Not married women.'

'Oh, leave her be, Ma. She was with her lord. Blame my brother for her lateness.'

Radha's long neck drooped and her head curved over her breast like a slender stem weighed down by the burden of a flower in full bloom. Never, she thought, with a shock of shame, had she felt with her husband the sensation that

Govinda's glance aroused. And his touch. A shudder con-
vulsed her as she recalled Govinda's finger, raising her face
to mirror his. Had he seen the passion reflected there?

It is profane and dishonourable, she told herself
staunchly. I love my husband. I am his handmaiden. He has
raised neither his hand nor his voice to me. His love makes
me safe and peaceful. This can't be love. I am restless,
ashamed and unhappy. I'm filled with him. His glance has
consumed me.

In the days that followed, Radha took a longer route home
from the fields where she visited her husband and milked the
cow. She was like a shadow of herself, a light imprint left in
the deep, dark forest. A radiant, flitting thing, weaving in
and out of the trees, her feet catching on trailing creepers.
Spring was everywhere and Vrindavan was a forest of love.
A dozen fragrances synthesized like an intoxicating mist.
And she, like the jasmine, wound herself around trees and
bushes, trying to catch a glimpse of Govinda unobserved.

Priya said, 'Go to him, Radha, my dear friend.'

But Radha was haughty in her anguish. 'He is always in
the arms of another woman.'

'Yet you stalk him? Do you hope to find him alone one
day? Is that why you try to glimpse him from behind the
leaves?'

At the thought of him Radha's body quivered, as the clove
creeper trembles when caressed by the sandalwood fragrance of the wind from the western ghats.

In spring when the mangroves came alive with their first
blossoms, the cuckoo burst into song. Radha was still seeking Govinda, tormented when she saw him, tortured when

she did not. She watched the forest burst into a rhapsody of love. Honey-bees scattered pollen in their wild love whirls from one bloom to another. Lovers, sheltering by night beneath the trees, sighed deeply, drinking in the passion of Madhuban, the Forest of Intoxication. Radha could hear them as she flitted wraith-like in the woods.

Through all of this, Priya said, 'Go to him, Radha. It is spring. The flame-tree's blooms are like the fingers of the love-god, clawing the breast of new love. The yellow *kesar* flower has opened like a golden umbrella. It is time for love. Time to flower.'

'And what of the *ketaka* pine?' Radha reminded her. 'The women plunder its flowers to entice Govinda.'

'I'll bring you the flowers of the *ketaka*, Radha, but go to Govinda. He loves you.'

In spite of herself Radha glanced at her friend. 'How do you know?'

'They all say that he has never before stopped playing his flute to greet someone. He has never offered anyone succour the way he did you. He has never left his ring of admirers to comfort a woman beyond it.'

Radha sniffed. 'Perhaps he has never had the chance.'

Priya became impatient. 'Then forget him.'

As she turned to walk away, Radha held her back. Her hand gleamed like a jasmine flower in the darkness of the forest. 'Don't go. I don't know what I want, why I search. I just know that Govinda is in my every breath.'

Priya seemed to expand and melt into the darkness. 'At last, you understand. Govinda is breath.'

For a moment, Radha looked up into Priya's face, then at the flowering *bakula* shrubs.

Priya followed her eyes. 'The flowers of love, so beautiful.'

Radha's breath was trapped in a sob. 'They say the *bakula* doesn't flower unless it's watered by the nectar of a young woman's mouth.'

Priya's eyes sparkled with mischief. 'Then it will bloom eternal in Vrindavan.' She laughed, but caught herself when she saw Radha's distress.

'You see, Priya? How can I risk everything for a man who flits like the bee from one flower to another?'

Priya held out her hand. 'Let us take the first step, Radha. Let us go to him.'

Radha felt strength course through her like the first summer swell of the Yamuna river. She grasped Priya's outstretched hand, then walked steadily, firm-footed, towards the mangrove to find Govinda.

The sight of him paralysed her. His head was sunk in the breast of a young woman. The skin of his neck and arms glistened with the sweat of passion. His shoulders heaved and his breath was laboured, lust-drunk. Another woman garlanded his neck with her arms. Yet another, giggling, ran up to him, whispering to him, then kissed his ear and nibbled the lobe. Govinda looked up, his eyelids heavy with desire. Radha knew he had seen her for he pinned her with an insolent gaze, yet he made no attempt to disentangle himself from the embraces of his lovers.

'So you came to me,' his gaze seemed to say. 'Who I am, how many lovers I take, none of it matters. Or that you have a husband. You came to me. I knew I could have you.'

Radha held his eye, unflinching. 'And now I will show you that I am not just like the others,' her eyes replied. Deliberately, she put down her pot and moved to a clear space. She tightened her mantle across her breasts and tucked it into the heavy golden belt at her waist. Then she began to dance, striking the ground with her lotus feet, her hands at her waist. In Madhuban, the Nectar Wood, she danced the dance of passion. In Madhuban, the Forest of Intoxication, she danced. The bells of her anklets struck up a melody of their own as her arms moved sinuously, drawing the veil over her face to defy his gaze. She danced – and Govinda played his flute. Faster, faster, to the strains of the music, she twirled and whirled. The veil fell from her doe eyes, and Radha danced.

See how she sways with passion, glowing golden, like her headband. Holding Govinda's gaze, she smiles sweetly, mischief and allure sparkling from within her. Radha dances and Govinda's flute flashes with her lightning moves – a beat for a beat, a pulse for a pulse. A drum pulsates from deep within the earth. It resounds through the forest, through the world, resonates within her.

My heart, she thinks, is the drum, my breath the drumbeat.

Her feet fly with the quickening tempo. Breath, movement, life-force twine into each other as her arms trace arabesques in the air. Then as suddenly and surely as she began, she comes to a stop, poised with one arm above her head, the other held like a lotus, forefinger and thumb pressed together, pointing skyward, the remaining three fingers gently curving.

Govinda continues to play. Bracelets jangle as hands clap. Radha is oblivious to the applause. Slowly, she brings her palms together with a bow of humility. Govinda takes the flute from his lips, and inclines his head. They are alone, locked in an unwavering gaze.

His dark-skinned body is swathed in a saffron robe, a forest garland draped around his sandal-dusted breast. His crown, decorated with peacock feathers, gleams in the forest darkness. His laughing face is intense now, the jewelled ear-rings glinting at his jaw. Radha draws his luminous beauty into her mind's eye, wraps it in her love, stores it away. Govinda the cowherd, the lover of milkmaids, love's tor-mentor, this is *her* Govinda.

'My Govinda,' her eyes say, defiant, 'if you have claimed me, I, too, have claimed you.'

'Then,' comes back the response of his eyes, 'nothing else matters.'

He moves towards Radha and she finds her feet pro-pelling her to him. No one else exists. They are two footsteps from each other when Radha realizes that the grove is empty. They are alone together. The next moment they are enfolded in each other's arms.

'Kuhu-kuhu!' the cuckoo calls, the erotic note, echoing the enraptured cry of Radha's heart.

There, in the grove of rushes and canes, Govinda coaxes Radha to the moist, tender grass. He makes her a bed of freshly sprouted greenery, lowers her on to a flower blanket and rests his head on her breast.

Radha lies very still, as if to hide the rage of longing. Govinda, too, is still. It seems an age before Radha's hands move, as if by their own will, wander to his soft hair and bury themselves in it. He raises his head, searches her face for invitation. Radha cries: 'Govinda.'

'That is the first time you've spoken my name,' he says.

Shyness overwhelms her.

He stretches out his body, hovering over her, limbs upon

limbs, face over face like a lean thundercloud about to pour forth its bounties on the parched ground.

'Radha, say my name again.'

She clenches her eyelids and turns away her face.

'Why so shy, my sweet one? Marriage should have made you a skilled lover.'

Radha's innocent eyes are filled with alarm. 'Skilled?' she murmurs.

Govinda throws back his head and laughs. 'The thousand guiles of innocence are more exciting to me than the fingers of the most skilled lover. You are married but you are still asleep. Shall I awaken you, my sweet? Shall I teach you the unforgettable?'

Radha is silent. Govinda pulls back, a half-smile on his lips, but his eyes are determined. Carelessly his hand strokes her bare skin. Radha says nothing.

'So you do not want me, after all?' Govinda begins to rise.

'No!' Radha cries. Govinda is standing now. Radha clutches his robes. 'Stay.'

'Why?'

'I want you to . . .'

'Want what?'

'I want you to . . . I want your love.' The words come in a rush.

'Radha!' Govinda falls to his knees. 'I will make love to you as the rain makes love to the earth. Look around you at the flowers of the Nectar Wood. It is the product of love's passion.'

As he speaks, his hands caress her limbs. Radha's skin is alive. Even the silken down on her limbs stirs and thrills to his touch. Govinda's lips touch hers, full, soft, warm. Radha moans softly. She can feel the tip of his tongue part her lips. She clings to him, pulling his body close to hers, feeling his weight on her as he takes his hands from her face. She is aware of his hands at her waist, undoing her golden girdle. 'Rest awhile, Jailer,' he murmurs, releasing the folds of her sari.

Radha gasps as she feels her naked skin beneath his fingers: the darkness of the forest is luminous. He will see her. Her husband has never seen her naked. Radha lets her eyelids quiver shut. Her body feels heavy, suddenly overcome with a languorous loss of inhibition.

If I die now, I will have been happier than any woman can imagine, she thinks.

'No talk of death, now,' Govinda replies.

She doesn't ask how he knows her thoughts. He hears her mind all the time – and she his. He rests his cheek against hers. Her skin is covered with a thin, sensual skin of liquid. She recognizes the same love-sheen on his body. Without thinking, she licks it from his neck. Clink! The chain of modesty snaps. Govinda snatches her in his arms and rolls over so that she is now above him, now below. He loosens the knot that holds her breasts imprisoned in their bodice and buries his face in them. Their laughter rings out loud and clear through the streams and falls of Vrindavan, across the roaring Yamuna and clear to the skies.

'Radha, I love you!' Govinda shouts.

'Govinda, I love you!' Radha coos.

'Your hair is covered in grass.' Govinda holds up her long tresses and lets them flow through his fingers like a waterfall darkened by the black rock behind it. He picks each blade of grass from her hair then lets it stream down again to her hips. He lays her down and arranges lotus blossoms along her. And all the while he admires her beauty. Now his gaze is fixed on her firm breasts.

She folds her arms over them.

Govinda pushes them away roughly and covers her breasts with his open palms. Radha pulls at his hands, and suddenly she gasps. Govinda has scratched her. She claws back but he is too swift for her, too practised in the games of love. He holds her wrists, raising them above his head like a triumphal arch. Radha struggles, then leans forward and nips his chest.

'Ah! Wild one!' Govinda lets go of her hands and lunges. Radha, her heart pumping in panic and passion, skips to her feet and runs with Govinda in pursuit. It is not long before he has caught her, swung her into his arms and brought her back to her bed of reeds and flowers.

They lie down, wet with exertion. Govinda takes her hand and lays it on his body. 'Prepare me for love,' he says softly.

Radha stares at him, suddenly timid again.

'Oh, my doe-eyed one,' he said, 'how little you know of the ways of pleasure.' He fastens her hand around his sarong and she begins slowly to disrobe him.

Suddenly she is troubled. 'The other girls . . .'

Govinda's eyes are closed in ecstasy as her fingers brush his skin. 'Which other girls?'

Radha pulls back. 'The *gopis*.'

Govinda does not reply.

Radha is distressed. 'Will you still make love to them?' She turns away to conceal her tears.

Govinda grasps her elbow. 'Radha, look at me.'

She does not.

He leans forward, turns her face forcibly as she struggles against his hand. 'You are all women to me. The One. There can never be anyone else.'

Radha weeps openly now. 'How can I believe you?'

Govinda strokes her hair and she rests her head on his shoulder, feeling his warmth. His tenderness suffuses her. His voice is soft as a cloud. 'Believe me because I speak the truth. I have at last found the One. Radha, my innocent, you are the soul of love.'

Radha sees the intensity of truth in his face. Her gaze wanders to the *bakula* flowers, starry against the leaves.

'Let the *bakula* trees be my witness,' Govinda says, so softly that his words are no more than breath on her skin. 'They will not bloom except when you are with me.'

She opens herself to him then, and flows towards him, merging in him. They rise and fall, entwine until they are so closely bound – two creepers, jasmine and clove – that it is impossible to tell which tendril belongs to which plant, where the flower blooms and where the spice. Now agitated, now calm, two entwined bodies in turn sway and grow still, plants in motion to the tune of the breezes.

Govinda's fingers linger on Radha's as she attempts to go. They barely touch her skin but their hold is powerful.

'The world is our enemy,' he whispers. 'It will try to keep us apart.'

'It cannot,' she replies. She sees in the depths of his eyes a certain knowing sadness. 'But I must go. My mother-in-law has been suspicious since the first time . . .'

Govinda smiles. 'Worldly ties are strong, sweet soul,' he murmurs. 'Look how they already bind you.'

Radha drops to her knees. She doesn't understand. Her

troubled eyes search his. 'They will not keep me away. I'll come to you at night. Tomorrow night when everyone is sleeping.'

'Perhaps,' Govinda replies. 'And I will wait for you here. But worldly bonds are hard to break. Love is strange. The world cannot exist without it, yet spurns it.'

Radha cradles her beloved in her arms. She had not known how hard it would be to take her leave. 'Nothing can keep me from you. Not now.'

'Ah, Radha, the soul is capable of anything once it knows the difference between Maya and Truth.'

Radha laughs. Her raven hair trembles and quivers, and the sunrays scatter across the Yamuna like tiny flames. 'I'm not clever enough to understand what you say,' she admits, 'but I know what I feel here.' She clasps his hand and brings it to the moist depth between her breasts.

Govinda lets his fist open and his fingers spread. 'And what do you feel *here*?' he challenges.

Radha blushes, veils her eyes with her thick lashes. 'I don't have words to explain,' she murmurs. 'I must go.'

Swiftly, she gathers up her skirts and her veil and runs through the forest, dipping beneath the familiar branches, skipping over the sharp rocks like a doe, slowing only as she approaches her husband's house.

Radha's mother-in-law was waiting for her, arms akimbo. 'Where have you been, my girl?' she demanded. 'And who is going to do your work?'

Her sister-in-law looked at her, aghast. 'Look at the state of you!'

Radha glanced down at her crumpled sari, her crushed

mantle. She could feel the love-tangles in her hastily knotted hair.

'What happened, Radhika?' the girl asked again.

'I fell,' Radha faltered. 'I stumbled in the woods and fell.'

'Where's the milk?'

'It fell too.'

'And the pot? I suppose you left that behind.'

'It was getting late. I was frightened. I'll go back and find it.'

The old woman darted forward and snatched Radha's shoulder. She dragged her into the inner courtyard. 'You'll do no such thing!' she rasped. 'You'll stay inside! Don't think I haven't noticed the change in you, skulking around half-demented. Your head's been in the clouds . . .'

Govinda's cloud-coloured skin floated into Radha's mind. A smile trembled on her lips.

'Are you mocking me? Shameless hussy! I can see through your tricks!'

She knows! Radha thought in alarm. She'll try to stop me. She'll tell Ayana.

'. . . Every daughter-in-law tries it at some point.' She clutched the bunch of keys at her waist, making a loud, dissonant jangle. 'You're trying to take these from me. But I waited long and worked hard to earn them. You will wait until I die.'

Radha was overwhelmed with relief. 'Keep your keys, Ma,' she whispered. 'I don't want them. I'm not ready to run the house. Maybe I never will be.'

Radha knew her husband believed none of the stories his mother told him: that Radha was trying to oust her; that Radha did none of the household tasks; that she didn't cook; that she didn't pray; that she never fasted for her husband.

But it hurt to know that he worried about her. He watched her distracted movements, her changing moods. He saw that her mind was never with him. He saw her clothes grow more and more dishevelled and her hair come loose, escaping like snakes from beneath her veil to guard her wild, tearless eyes. And he grieved for the serenity that had gone from her beautiful face, leaving behind torment. He knew something was amiss. Yet Radha asked for nothing and denied nothing. Like a lost, deprived soul, she did as she was told without protest. 'We'll move across the river,' his mother said. 'Radha is bewitched.'

'Radha?' her husband said. 'Mother wants us to move across the river.'

'Yamuna, Sister of Death,' Radha replied, dull-voiced. 'As you wish.'

Across the Yamuna – across the great river from Govinda.

Well, what difference would it make? He had not called to her again since that night. He had never come to see her, sent her no messages. She was just one of the many women to whom he made daily pledges. The night she had gone back to him, her heart beating with passion after three days of being watched by her mother-in-law, she had seen him surrounded by women. There he sat, playing a tune of love-longing on his flute, as women sported and danced around him. Just as before, some kissed him, some made as if to slip, an excuse to lean on him for support. And he played for them on his flute, compelling them to dance to his tune. And he had made her part of it. He had deceived her.

Radha wanted to forget but he possessed her mind, was entrenched in her heart like the sharp stone in the heart of a peach. He was like a fire burning away her senses, flickering and blazing in her mind. How could she think of anything other than the burning when she was on fire? She could douse herself in water, roll in the moist grass. But that would not help her: the fire was unreachable, unassailable. So she resigned herself to burning. If only the cruel flames would consume her instead of lingering, licking her slowly, nerve by nerve. She saw them as the funeral pyre of her love, her ruthless, jealous lord. So she burned day and night, in an agony of jealousy. Yes, perhaps that Sister of Death, the river who had watched her union with Govinda, would quench the fire. Perhaps she would pull Radha in, lap her in embraces, rock her to sleep.

Priya rushed in. 'Why are you going to live on the other side of the river?'

Radha shrugged, languid. 'They decided.'

'But what about Govinda?'

Some of the fire flashed in Radha's eyes. 'I am nothing to him.'

'Radha, he loves you.'

Radha put her arms around Priya. 'My sweet friend, I know you love me, but what is the use of false hopes? I saw him, surrounded with women as before.'

'Then I'll go to him. I've been in Vrindavan as usual and for weeks I've not heard the flute, nor seen the *gopis*. It's wretched there, like a wilderness.'

Radha's eyes grew dreamy. 'He's with another of the thousand Radhas, playing alone in some secret place. But she is luckier than I for she has been with him many days.'

Her eyes filled and overflowed. Priya cradled Radha's head against her shoulder. 'Don't!' she whispered urgently. 'Don't torment yourself. I will go to him. I came to tell you that I found him. He was in the same space beside the Yamuna where he took you to make love.'

'I told him you had seen him, surrounded by *gopis*, and gone away heartbroken. Your Govinda bowed his head, but not before I saw the shame in his eyes. "I know," he replied. "I waited so long for Radha – for three nights she did not come to me. And I knew that the pull of worldly things was more powerful than my love. The girls came, they surrounded me, I played for them and let them try to entertain me with dancing and laughter. But there was no charm left in them, no nectar in their lips, no allure in their eyes. Once, as they walked past me, their arms raised above their heads revealing their breasts, my arms lifted, the flute found my lips, my breath infused it and I made music. But I had placed Radha in my heart, and desire for others was dispelled. I have looked for Radha everywhere. My mind is weak with arrow-wounds of love. The lush fertility of the forest makes me grieve, the entwined vines fill me with loneliness. Even the scented breezes rising off the lotus ponds offend me with their touch. My body is Radha's, and only hers, so I stay in the grove, lamenting, hoping that one day she might come back to me."'

'Why have you sent her no message?' Priya had asked, tears flowing down her cheeks.

'If Radha truly loves me, she knows I love her too. Ah, Priya. No lover may seek unless the beloved desires to be found. It is a commandment of love.'

'But she does desire it! When she saw you with the *gopis*, she was torn with jealousy. But she waited for a love-call from your flute. There was nothing. What was she to think, Govinda?'

Govinda's eyes were wild. 'What message was I to send to her? Who might read it before her? Would she ever receive it?'

'So,' Priya concluded, 'I offered to be the messenger of sweet Govinda. He sent you this song, but he told me to sing it only if I was sure of your feelings for him. "Love demanded, is love degraded," he said. "If Radha comes, it must be because she seeks me as I seek her."'

'Tell me, Priya, I'm impatient to know how he deceived you.'

Govinda said, 'I imagine her anger in her face. I see her brow curved with rage like the red lotus, tormented by a bee. She's gone from me. But she's merged in me, and there I make love to her every moment. What makes me seek her in the forest? What makes me call to her? Oh, slender woman! I understand your dismay. I cannot give you back your peace because you have exiled yourself from me. Forgive me! Grant me a glimpse of you! I'm consumed with passion. The ecstasy of your touch, your innocent eyes, the lotus-fragrance of your breath, the nectar of your teasing words. Oh, Radha, if only you knew, you are my meditation, my most sacred prayer. Yet the pain of loss keeps growing.'

Then Govinda played the flute for the first time in an age. 'I will play for Radhika,' he said. The waves of his melody surged towards the moon, where he saw your face. Scattered through Mathura, all the *gopis* heard and overflowed with sadness for unfulfilled love.

Priya stroked Radha's wild tresses. 'Go, my friend, to the dark grove, conceal yourself in a midnight cloak. The wind is gentle where he waits. But he asked me to remind you of these words: "Love demanded, is love degraded. If Radha comes, it must be because she seeks me as I seek her."'

Govinda's song suffused Radha with fresh life. 'Is he questioning my love, Priya, after he saw me come to him? Knowing the risks I had taken? Yes, I'll go to him – not to answer to his demands but because I love him.'

Radha walked swiftly to the door. The bells of her anklets clinked and jangled. In past days they had been capricious enemies, reporting her every movement to the other women in the house.

Priya said, 'Hush, Radha! Your mother-in-law will stop you if she hears.'

'No one can stop me now. These anklets have bound me too fast. Worldly ties have constrained me too long. I have lain awake at night watching the moon. It spreads fire through my body. I grow hot and fevered here. I'm going now where I might gain what I desire.'

Distracted, desperate, Radha followed the path to Govinda's grove. Could Priya's words have been true? She had said: 'The one who wears the forest garland awaits. The *bakula* flowers are dead. Govinda seems to die too, consumed by the cool rays of the moon. Alone, sad . . . he is in the love-shrine, waiting. Thoughts of you keep him alive. He meditates on you, yearns for the dew of your embraces.'

Radha walked on. She noticed that the *bakula* flowers hung in clusters, withered or wilting amid lustrous foliage. No maidens had tended them. Could it be that Govinda had kept his promise to her? But no, she could not let herself believe that. There might be another reason for the plight of the *bakula*. She paused a moment, orienting herself. Where was she? Stopping to take stock confused her: as long as she had let her feet follow her instinct she had been sure of her direction. Now, suddenly, she didn't know which way to turn.

But wait now . . . Govinda is calling to her heart. The soul knows which way to go. His breath fills all of Vrindavan with longing. His flute sings of Radha. 'O breeze from the western ghats, O scented sandalwood breeze that touches her body, touch me too so that I can feel my Radha again.'

She follows the call of the flute, breathing the air Govinda is exhaling. Soon she recognizes her surroundings. Any moment now, she will see him.

She rests against a tree, stretched to her full height, her head against its trunk. 'O Love!' she cries. 'If he does not want me, take my life. I shall never seek refuge at home again. Death's Sister, moisten my limbs with waves. Quench the fire in my body.'

She steps into the glade.

Govinda looks at her, still and silent. Only his eyes speak. 'Radha, sweet soul, you are here at last.'

But Radha's armour is strong. It repels love's words. In the cloud-colour of his skin she sees the smudged kohl of beautiful maiden-eyes. His lips, she believes, are dark and full from their kisses. Where his skin has been scratched by the twigs and thorns, she sees the lacerations of love play.

Anger leaps within her. Why had she come here to confirm what she already knew?

'Don't lie to me, or your inner self will become as dark as the outer. How can you lure me here, then betray me? You filled me with wonder, Govinda, but I was right. You wander in the forest to devour women.' She advances on him like a warrior unafraid of death.

Still Govinda does not speak.

'I feel more shame than anguish at being deceived by you. But your magical laughter mesmerizes. You are the arch-deceiver.'

Govinda bows his head, acquiescent. 'But it is in the past.' He falls to his knees.

'If only I could believe you!' Radha sees herself floating in the Yamuna, Sister of Death, oblivious, body separated from soul, free at last. She sees her hair tumbling around her.

Govinda smiles sadly. 'Look at your hair – untended in your grief. Why must you torment yourself, Radha? Hear me out.'

'So that you may hurt me again? I can never trust you, Govinda.'

'Ah, this Love, he drives the best of us to illogical behaviour. When the beloved is tender, Radha, you are rough. When I bend down, you are inflexible. Now I am passionate, you are hostile. I raise my face to you, but you turn away.'

Radha steps back as she feels her arms demand to place themselves around his head and hold him close.

'Your sweet sandalwood perfume is like a poison now, the cool moon-lustre of your face is burning me like the noonday sun, roasting me in its flames. The pleasures of my love are like threats of torture. Frost is flame.'

Radha is speechless. Govinda is inside her. Once again he is touching her essence. He *knows* the flood of emotions surging and thrashing inside her, wild waves of Death's Sister in a tempest.

Wave by wave, her grief begins to calm. Govinda's words are like a cooling breeze that penetrates her body, reaching deep inside. And when he bows his head at her feet she falls to her knees with a cry. She wants to embrace him – instead she grips his shoulders, thrusting him away. He falls back, unresisting and she finds herself astride him, scratching at his chest, striking with her fists. Govinda encloses her in a firm embrace, steady and safe, until the anger dies down and she lies on him, still and exhausted, all resistance gone as her soul casts off physical restraints and is liberated. Now, at last, she understands. There is no separation from him. They clench each other in a wild embrace.

You'll be like a necklace on my chest, like a fluttering crane above me, like lightning in a thundercloud, my golden woman. You'll shine as you make love, astride me. Place your hips now, on mine ungirdled, unbound, uncovered. Here the mind is gentle. There is nothing but love.

Now he is the smooth flowing body of the Yamuna, she the proliferating ripples on its surface, they are the river in Oneness. And there, in the waters of their sweet exertions, they lie, fulfilled for eternity.

Amaltheia and Chryse

Just when I was about to abandon my search for an occasion when Zeus showed tenderness towards women, I found Harry Robin's delicious tales describing the initiation of the boy Zeus.

Amaltheia

I had reached my fourteenth summer. Amaltheia had taught me the stories of the Beginning, the names of the old gods and goddesses, the names of trees, flowers, birds, and snakes; the habits of wild and tameable animals; and how to read and write. Amaltheia's delight in knowledge kindled my own, and refined my senses and memory.

Every morning Amaltheia brought a milk goat to the cave. As I watched her gentle hands tugging at the goat's teats I would sense a slow, pleasurable stirring in my phallos. One morning I moved to stand close behind her while she was milking the goat. Blindly unable to resist the impulse, I cupped her breasts in my hands. Almost immediately I felt the delicious shock of her nipples hardening in my palms.

While she continued to milk the goat, she turned to smile at me over her shoulder and said,

'Zeus, you are not quite ready to fulfil what you desire.'

I swiftly took my hands away, with the forms of her breasts and nipples warm and glowing in my palms. When she saw my flushed face she said,

'You didn't harm me, don't be sad!' and then she turned back to the goat's teats.

Later that summer, at twilight one day, a heavy wind began to churn the water offshore. Then low, rolling clouds chased themselves over the beach, racing up and over the hillsides to envelope Mount Ida. The twilight was swiftly transformed into dense, black night. A drenching rain began to fall after we had gone to our beds.

My bedroom in the cave was in an enclosed alcove, close to the cave's entrance. Lightning flickered through the heavy cloths that hid the cave's mouth, and the thunder's snapping and booming prevented sleep.

Suddenly, in a crackling flare of lightning, Amaltheia ran into my bedroom. Shivering and frightened by the wild storm, she asked if she might share my bed until the lightning and thunder had spent themselves.

I welcomed her. We lay quietly on our backs, not touching, listening to the fury of the wind and the rain and the long rolls of thunder, while I sensed our heat mingling under the sheepskin cover. The storm grew noisier and wilder, making sleep impossible.

Amaltheia whispered that it seemed a propitious time to teach me about male and female. I left the bed to light a torch and swiftly returned to her side. She pulled the hem of her sea-green nightdress up to her armpits. Slowly and patiently, she showed me how to caress her face, her shoulders, her white breasts and red nipples, the rich black hair of her armpits and pubes, and the ivory skin of her buttocks, her thighs, calves, ankles and feet.

Then she guided my forefinger to touch the moist little horn – she called it her klitoris – in the cleft between her legs. She gasped, and cautioned me to be ever slow and gentle. When she offered her breasts to my lips I kissed them and sucked at her nipples, driving away all thought, transforming my mind into a temple of pure, luxurious thirst.

I continued to caress her klitoris while she began, lightly and slowly, to palm and finger the loose skin at the top of my burning phallos. We moaned our pleasures while the storm raged ever louder, until she cried out at the very instant that my phallos exploded, rocking my body like the oaks I had seen splitting under the lightning bolts. She shivered while I heard myself gasping and groaning with the power of my spurtings. She would not allow me to thrust my phallos into her konnos, she said, because she loved and wanted only Melisseos, her husband, for what she called the *ultimate caress*.

I asked her to remove her nightdress so that I could study her body. Then I slowly rubbed her skin with a rough cloth, to prolong my pleasure. She smiled when she saw my phallos engorged again. The lightning and thunder diminished as the storm moved westward, so we embraced silently and gratefully before we went to our separate beds.

Before I fell asleep I thought of Gaia. Was that exquisite encounter with Amaltheia another secret gift she had sent to me? Suddenly I saw how Gaia, our Mother Earth, might impregnate herself! She could invoke Kronos to make a storm! Lightning bolts would penetrate her body wherever they struck. And those roaring, rolling thunders were simply the passionate moans and gasps, like Amaltheia's and my own, of Gaia's mounting, peaking, and waning tensions. I slept soundly that night.

Chryse

Early next morning, I went to the mouth of my cave just as the Sun began to streak the fading night sky with pink and gold. I sensed my body smiling with the memory of Amaltheia. I watched my friend, the hawk who visited the hillside above my cave every day, searching for his breakfast, playing on the gusts of wind with his great wings.

The shape of the beach had changed during the stormy night. But the low, rolling waves enticed me. Disregarding the rules designed for my safety, I ran down to the shore and dived into the water. It was very cold, but I could have drunk the entire sea in my joyous state.

Captain Ilos came running down to the shore, waving furiously at me to get out of the water. I did so. I saw his lips twitching between sternness and affection. He pointed up to the cave and said, 'Zeus, go!'

I suppressed my laugh at his command – 'Zeus, go!' – and we ran up the slope and into the cave.

Ilos quietly scolded me for breaking the rule that I must not wander away from the cave without a guard. I stopped him with a wave of my hand and said,

'Thank you, I shall be more careful. I'm hungry, will you join me?'

We ate together, at ease in our friendship.

Later I lay on my back just inside the mouth of the cave, relishing the sky, the beach, and the colors of the sea. Amaltheia had taught me the pleasant-sounding words for those colors: azure, amethyst, crimson, emerald, sapphire, chrysoprase.

I heard the sound of Amaltheia's sandals and smelled her scent as she came closer. She halted just behind my head. I turned to look up to her upside-down, smiling eyes.

She said, 'Zeus, I must talk with you.'

I arose and followed her to my alcove. She had put my room in order; there was no sign of the night's encounter. We sat facing each other in the cushioned chairs.

Amaltheia seemed more beautiful than ever before. She closed her eyes, silently collecting herself for what she was about to say. When she opened them and looked at me I quivered with the brief shock of their brilliant green. She spoke with an odd, trembling undertone. I had a fleeting thought that she might break into tears, but she didn't.

'Zeus! We have been friends ever since you were a little child. You have reached your maturity, as we both know after last night.

'Now you must learn the ultimate caress. You are surprised. I expected that, but please allow me to continue, don't interrupt. You already know why I will not allow you that with me.

'So I have asked one of our nymphs, Chryse, to teach you that caress. Chryse is barren —'

I interrupted to ask, 'Barren? What does that mean?'

'It means that she cannot bring children into the world. Some women will be barren all their lives. Chryse has had lovers, but she has never conceived a child. So you will be able to enjoy her teaching without making a child.

'I must also tell you that she was pleased to be chosen for that task.'

I remember Amaltheia's little smile as she said, *'that task'*.

'Chryse will come to your alcove tonight, when the rest of us are asleep. She will be bathed and perfumed, so I ask that you too bathe this evening. I must remind you to be gentle, and to be attentive to whatever she may wish. Please do not ask more questions. I shall see you tomorrow, of course.'

Again she smiled. Then she arose and walked swiftly away.

At nightfall I lit a torch in the far corner of my alcove. I intended to see Chryse without the cloak of darkness. I washed and rubbed myself dry, dressed in a thin robe, and lay down to wait for her.

Although I had seen each of the nymphs who worked in my cave-palace on one or another occasion, I hadn't learned their names. They always worked silently at their tasks, and they always averted their eyes in my presence. I tried to remember each of their faces as I resisted falling asleep.

The hissing sound of sandals on the stone floor brought me fully awake. The nymph halted at the entrance to my alcove. I could see that she was shivering slightly, although she was covered from the top of her head to her bare ankles in a thick sheepskin hood and cloak.

She took a deep breath to control her chattering teeth and said,

'I am Chryse. You are waiting for me.'

I arose from my bed and whispered, 'Come closer, do not be afraid.'

She stepped forward. She was quite tall, the top of her head reaching just below the level of my shoulders. Now I could see only her soft golden eyes and lashes. Some strands of hair had escaped from her hood.

I smiled and asked, 'May I see your face, Chryse?'

She did not reply. It seemed as if the night would pass before she whispered,

'It would please me if you uncovered me.'

I said nothing. I had never seen her before now, so she must have come from the palace at Timbakion. Her long, golden hair spilled out when I lifted the hood and cloak from her shoulders and let it fall to the floor. She was naked. She lowered her eyes to avoid mine, and intertwined her fingers over her belly.

I had never seen anyone so beautiful.

I said, 'Chryse, look at me.'

She did so, with a little smile curving her lips. I held my gaze to her eyes while I slowly touched her neck, her shoulders, her arms. I cupped her breasts and fingered the pink nipples pressing out of them. I moved my hand to her hips, tasting her skin with my fingertips. Then, grasping her hips, I made her turn her back to me.

I moved my fingers down from the nape of her neck, tracing her shoulders, her arms, and the hollow flowing down the center of her back to her waist into the cleft between the half-moons of her buttocks. I shivered when I felt her heat enveloping my hand.

My stiffened phallos thrusted at the front of my robe, as if it were seeking into her shadowed cleft, but she turned around to say that she would disrobe me. She shook in little spasms while she squatted to grasp the hem of my robe. She lifted it slowly and paused to stare at my phallos.

She whispered, 'Raise your arms,' and pulled my robe over my head. We moved closer, naked, smiling into each other's eyes while the tip of my phallos quivered in the soft, golden hair of her pubes.

I whispered, 'How beautiful you are, Chryse!'

She smiled into my eyes as she deftly pulled back the sheath of my phallos to expose its crown. She enclosed it in her soft palm, still gazing into my eyes.

'How wonderful you are, Zeus!'

'Shall we warm ourselves?'

She immediately replied, 'Yes,' went to my bed and pulled the sheepskin to cover herself to her nose. I could see her eyes smiling at me while she shivered under the sheepskin cover. I took the torch, set fire to the wood in the brazier and brought it close to the bed. I felt her eyes follow my movements around the alcove.

I returned to the bed and removed the sheepskin so that I might study her nakedness. She surely sensed my wish for she slowly turned to lie on her back.

She stretched her legs, pressing them together, and folded her arms under her head to make an image that burned itself into my brain, the image of the female awaiting the delirium and ecstasy that she and the male can offer each other. I understood now that Chryse was at ease with herself, with her talent for giving and receiving pleasure.

I lay down close to her and brought her face to face, belly

to belly, so that our noses almost touched. When I smelled her spiced breath I brushed her lips with mine. I had never known a kiss!

She smiled and whispered, 'I shall call that the moth's kiss. This is the bee's kiss,' and she gently moved her tongue to taste and open my lips and search in the corners of my mouth. She moved her hand below my phallos to cup my heavy testicles. Then she encircled my phallos with her palm and fingers and slowly stroked its sheath up and down until my hot juices erupted. I groaned with the pure pleasure of her touch.

She whispered, 'Yes, and this is how you will move when you have entered me.' She palmed some of my juice from her belly and resumed stroking my phallos, holding it more tightly than before.

'And this is what you will feel when my juices flow.'

I kissed her soft mouth with the bee's kiss while my tremors subsided. We lay intertwined, silent, resting.

Again she whispered, 'Your testicles will be filled again, soon. And because you have already released those waiting juices, you will be able to enter and caress my konnos for a much longer time. I was not prepared for such sweet pleasure with you. I know that you are a god. So I shall do whatever you ask, to make you remember me for all your days and nights.'

I pulled up the sheepskin and we slept for a while.

I awakened with my phallos erect and throbbing again. I studied her golden hair and the glistening, golden lashes of her closed eyelids. She opened her eyes to look at me, and I could see her sleep dissolving.

'Now?' she said.

I whispered, 'Yes.'

She asked me to leave the bed and remove the sheepskin.

Now lying on her back, she extended her arms to me while she slowly opened her legs wide and raised her buttocks so that I could see the moist, golden hairs that barely concealed the secret of her konnos. Then she slowly brought her legs together, and bent her knees. Raising her hips, she extended her legs, made a slight fluttering gesture with her toes and said, 'Now.'

I understood that she wished me to place my shoulders under her knees so that my chest and groin would touch the back of her thighs and her buttocks when I entered her. I did so, as slowly as I could control my quivering body. She gently pulsed her hips, helping me to move deeper and deeper into her until my phallos became the root and trunk of my being.

I brushed her breasts, locked my arms around her thighs, and began the motion of all males in the pursuit of godship, while she rocked her hips to match the rhythms of my blind caressing to move with me into the luminous throes of orgasm.

I licked her back, tasting the delicious salt of our mingled sweat. She slowly slid her legs down my wet arms and whispered, 'Please stay, don't withdraw.'

Her cheeks were wet with tears. I kissed her with the bee's kiss.

While our breathing grew calmer I could feel the slow engorging of my phallos again, now deep and voluptuous within her. I wanted to know everything now. What I could not see, I would touch.

She smiled with pleasure when I moved my finger to caress the entrance to her konnos. I grasped her buttocks and pinched and stroked them, then I moved my hands under her back to caress her muscles and spine. She closed her eyes, imagining my finger's searchings. When I touched a pleasurable place she suddenly opened her eyes, startled and unseeing. In those moments her eyes became deep, golden oceans.

Enveloped in her konnos, motionless, my phallos throbbed, impatient. She sighed deeply again.

As if by their own will my hips moved again into the ultimate caress. Chryse's eyes opened wider as my thrusting grew more and more forceful. She gripped my shoulders and raised her head to stare at our coupling. When she offered up her mouth to mine in a delirious kiss we erupted together like twin volcanoes, gasping and moaning. We collapsed into spacious sleep.

I awakened just before dawn and gently brought her awake, ascending with her into a different, utterly sweet climax. I, a god, and Chryse, a nymph, had been – too briefly! – transformed into our essences, male and female. We sank into sleep again.

I guided her to sit on my lap close to the brazier and rubbed her wonderful skin with a warm cloth. She clasped her hands in the mass of her hair and raised her arms, revealing the secret, golden fronds in her armpits, burning the image of her nudity into my memory.

I asked if she would visit me again. She cupped and softly rubbed my testicles. I fondled and kissed her breasts until she replied, 'Yes, whenever you wish.' She smiled while I helped her into her cloak. We looked into each other's eyes silently, and kissed lightly, the moth's kiss – before she turned to walk out of my cave.

The calm sea beyond my cave mirrored the pinks and pale blues of the sky at early dawn.

Chryse! Unforgettable, beautiful Chryse!

The Vernal Palace

I was highly amused by this tongue-in-cheek account of how a scholar, skilled in sex-craft, used a manual complete with pictures to liberate a modest virgin from her inhibitions.

The young man bade his servants seek out all the marriage brokers they could find and commission them to search the city and countryside for the most beautiful of marriageable girls. She must be of respectable and distinguished family; and he insisted that she must be not only beautiful, but intelligent and well educated as well. There was no lack of offers. Each day a number of marriage brokers came to him with their suggestions. Where the candidate was not too high in the social scale, the matchmaker would bring her along to be introduced and inspected at first hand. But in the case of a distinguished family which insisted on its forms and observances, she arranged to have the young man, as though by chance, cross the young lady's path in the courtyard of one of the temples, or while she was taking the air outside the city walls.

All these meetings and tours of inspection proved useless. A certain number of worthy young persons were unnecessarily

jolted out of their peaceful routines and sent home again with
vain pangs in their tender little hearts. For of all the candidates
who were brought forward, not one met with the exacting
suitor's approval.

But one of the marriage brokers said to the young man:
'Now, it is clear to me that among all the young candidates
there is only one who is worth considering: Miss Noble
Scent; her father is a private scholar, known throughout the
city by the surname T'ieh-fei tao-jen, Iron Door Follower of
the Tao. She alone can meet your stringent requirements.
But in her case there is a difficulty: her father is an old crank
who adheres rigidly to the ancient customs. He would certainly not permit you to inspect his daughter before
marriage. Consequently I fear that even this last hope must
be abandoned.'

'Iron Door Follower of the Tao? How did he come by
such a strange surname? Why does he not wish his daughter
to be seen? And if he keeps her hidden from all eyes, how do
you know she is beautiful?'

'As I have told you, the old gentleman is rather crochety;
he cares only for his books and avoids all society. He doesn't
see a living soul. He lives in a splendid country house outside
the city, with fields and meadows round it. He is a wealthy
widower and his daughter is his only child. As for her
beauty, it is no exaggeration to liken her to a lovely flower, a
precious jewel. In addition, her father has given her an excellent education and her little head is full of learning. Her
upbringing, as you may easily surmise, has been extremely
strict, and she has hardly ever set foot outside her maidenly
quarters. She never goes out, not even to the traditional serv-
ices on temple holidays. She is sixteen years old and has

never been seen in public. Even we three go-betweens and six marriage brokers have no wings, we can't fly into her living quarters. It was only by the purest accident that I myself caught a glimpse of her not long ago.

'Yesterday I chanced to pass the house while the old gentleman was standing outside the door. He stopped me and asked if I were not Mother Liu, whose trade it was to arrange marriages. When I answered in the affirmative, he invited me in and presented his daughter. "This is the young lady, my only child," he said, and continued: "Now I should like you to look around and bring me a suitable son-in-law who is worthy of her and has the qualities he would need to be a son to me and the prop of my old age." At once I suggested that the young gentleman would be an appropriate match. He said: "I have already heard of him, he is said to possess high intellectual gifts as well as external advantages. But what of his character and his virtue?" To this I replied: "The young gentleman is distinguished by a spiritual and ethical maturity far in advance of his years. His character is without the slightest blemish or weak point. There is only one thing: he absolutely insists on seeing his future bride with his own eyes before the betrothal." At once the benevolent look vanished from the old gentleman's face, and he became very angry: "Nonsense. He wants to see her first – that may be permissible in the case of a venal powder-puff, a rutting mare from Yangchow. But since when is it the custom to expose the honorable daughter of a good family to the eyes of a strange man? A fine thing that would be. An impudent demand, which makes it clear to me that the young man is not the right husband for my daughter. Not another word!" With this he broke off the interview and sent me on my way. So you see, young man, there is nothing more to be done.'

The young man thought the matter over carefully.

'If I were to marry this beautiful young girl and take her into my own house, there would be no one but me – for I am without parents or brothers – to keep an eye on her. I should have to stay home all day guarding her, there would be no chance whatever to go out. But if I went to live in her house, there would be no such difficulty, for this ancient guardian of virtue, my father-in-law, would keep a good watch over her in my absence. I should be able to go out with an easy heart. The only point that bothers me is not to see her first. What confidence can I have in a matchmaker's prattle? Why, there's no limit to what her kind will say in praise of a possible match.' Such were his thoughts. To Mama Liu he said:

'If I am to believe you, she would be an excellent wife, yes, just the right wife for me. I should just like to ask you this one thing: to find some way of my getting the merest glimpse of her and hearing the sound of her voice. Then if the general impression is favorable, the match is made.'

'See her first? It's out of the question. But if you don't trust me, why not go to a soothsayer and consult the little straws of fate?'

'There you have given me a very good idea. I have a friend who is an expert at conjuring spirits and telling fortunes, and his predictions have always been confirmed. I shall ask his advice. Let us wait to see what fate decides. Then I shall send for you and tell you what has happened.'

So it was agreed and Mama Liu departed.

Next day the young man fasted and bathed and asked his friend the diviner to his house for a consultation. In the house-temple lit by candles and filled with incense, he solemnly explained the business in hand, humbly bowing his head and speaking in a muffled voice as though praying to a higher being.

'The younger brother has heard of the unsurpassed beauty of Miss Noble Scent, daughter of Iron Door Follower of the Tao, and would like to take her for his wife. But only his ears have heard of her charms, his eyes have not seen them. Therefore he begs leave to ask the exalted spirit whether she is indeed so beautiful and whether the exalted spirit recommends a marriage with her. If there should be even the slightest blemish in her, he would prefer to abandon the idea of marrying her. He fervently implores the exalted spirit to give him some gracious hint, for he does not wish to forfeit all happiness by trusting in idle prattle.'

After stating his request, he made the fourfold sign on his forehead in reverence to the unknown spirit. Rising once more to his feet, he took from his friend's hand a piece of wood from the magic *luan* tree, symbolizing the spirit, held it chest high, and waited with bated breath to see what would happen next. Then he heard a sound, as of a brush passing softly over paper. A pluck at his sleeve awakened him from his trance. His friend was holding out a sheet of paper. On it was written a quatrain:

Number 1:

> No need to doubt this message of the spirits:
> She is first in the grove of red flowers.
> Yet there is cause for alarm. So much beauty attracts
>   suitors.

Whether the marriage is happy or not – is a question
of morality.

The young man reflected: 'It is clear then that she is a
first-class beauty. That is the main thing. As for the second
part of the communication, it does not mince words about
the danger such beauty involves. Can it be that the melon
has already been cut open? No, that is very unlikely. Let us
wait and see what the second communication says. There
must be another since the first one is headed 'Number 1'.

Again he held out the magic wood, then again he heard
rustling and received the second communication, which ran:

It would be presumptuous to bank on your wife's
fidelity;
Accordingly, if the husband values domestic harmony,
He will lock the gates and not admit a fly.
The tiniest fly-dropping will spoil a jewel.

> Written by Hui-tao-jen
> the returned follower of the Tao

The three ideograms Hui-tao-jen were familiar to our
young man: as he knew, they spelled the surname behind
which the Taoist patriarch Lü Shun-yang (Lü Yen, also
known as Lü Tung-pin, b. 750 AD) had hidden; he was also
acquainted with the patriarch's life and personality; in his
time, the young man recalled to his satisfaction, he had been
a great devotee and connoisseur of wine and women. So, it
was *his* spirit that had entered into his friend during the
séance and guided the brush. There could be no doubt that
the spirit approved his choice.

He made a bow of thanks toward the empty air, intended for the spirit of the patriarch Lü Shun-yang. Then he sent for Mama Liu, the marriage broker.

'The spirit has spoken in favor of my marriage with Miss Noble Scent. A personal inspection is not necessary. Go quickly and settle the details.' Thus dismissed, Mama Liu made all haste to the house of Dr Iron Door, and informed him that her client no longer insisted on previous inspection of his bride-to-be.

'But he did at first,' Dr Iron Door grumbled, 'and by so doing showed himself to be deplorably superficial, the kind of man who attaches more importance to externals than to superior character. He is not the son-in-law for me. I must have a man of the utmost moral rigor, who takes a thoroughly serious view of life.'

Intent on her fee, Mama Liu summoned up all her ingenuity to overcome his resistance:

'If he wished at first to see the young lady, his only motive was one of kindness and tact. He was afraid that she might be too frail and delicate for married life. Once I was able to set his mind at rest, he was overjoyed to hear how strictly and carefully she had been raised, and how, thanks to your guidance, she had become a veritable epitome of maidenly virtue. That decided him, and he bade me intercede with you to honor him by taking him into your worthy house.'

Flattered at these remarks, Dr Iron Door nodded his approval. Then it was a sense of delicacy that made him wish to see her first? And it was her sound upbringing that had decided him? That sounded sensible and argued very much in the young man's favor. And he gave his paternal consent.

❖

And so on a lucky calendar day the young man was received in Dr Iron Door's home, and with Noble Scent on the carpet beside him, made the traditional bows to heaven and earth, ancestors and father-in-law. At nightfall when he was at last alone with her in the bridal chamber and she lifted her veil, he fixed his eyes upon his bride in feverish expectation. For to the last moment a doubt had lurked in a corner of his heart; to the last moment he had thought that Mama Liu's assurance must be slightly exaggerated, a product as it were of poetic license. But now that he was able to view her close at hand, in the full light of the lamps and candles, his heart leapt with delight. Her beauty exceeded his wildest expectations.

Unquestionably Noble Scent was a peerless beauty, but to her partner's grief she was an utter failure at the 'wind-and-moon game' and the hopes with which he had looked forward to his wedding night remained at least seven-tenths unfulfilled. Small wonder. Thanks to the traditional upbringing she had received from her strict, ultra-conservative parents, she wore an armor of virginal modesty and reserve, against which his tender assaults bounded off without the slightest effect. He was quite dismayed at her lack of response to his advances. If he allowed his language to become even mildly daring or frivolous, she blushed and took flight. He liked to play the 'wind-and-moon game' not only at night but also in broad daylight, for it seemed to him that his pleasure was very much increased by the possibility of looking at certain secret parts of the body. On several occasions he attempted, in the morning or afternoon, to insert a bold hand beneath her clothing and to strip off her undermost coverings. The reception was not what he had bargained for. She resisted vigorously and screamed as though threatened with rape. At night, to be sure, she permitted his embraces, but quite apathetically as though merely doing her duty. He had to stick to the stodgy ancestral method, and any attempt at more modern, more refined variations met with fierce opposition. When he attempted the 'fetching fire behind the hill' position, she said it was perfectly disgusting and contrary to all the rules of husbandly behavior. When he tried the 'making candles by dipping the wick in tallow' position, she protested that such goings-on were utterly nasty and vulgar. It took all his powers of persuasion even to make her prop up her thighs on his shoulders. When their pleasure approached a climax, not the tiniest little cry, not the slightest moan of happiness was to be heard from her. Even when he smothered her in tender little cries of 'My heart, my liver', or 'My life, my everything', she took no more interest than if she had been deaf and dumb. It was enough to drive him to despair. He began to make fun of her and to call her his 'little saint'.

'Things can't go on like this. I must find some way of educating her and ridding her of those awful moral inhibitions – the best idea would be some stimulating reading matter.' So saying, he repaired to the booksellers' quarter. There, after a long search he procured a marvellously illustrated volume entitled *Ch'un-t'ang*, 'The Vernal Palace'. It was a celebrated book on the art of love, written by no less a man than the Grand Secretary, Tzu-ang. It included thirty-six pictures, clearly and artfully illustrating the thirty-six different 'positions' of vernal dalliance, of which the poets of the T-ang period had sung. He brought the book home with him and handed it to the 'little saint'. As they leafed through page after page, he whispered to her:

'You see that I haven't been asking you to join in any monkey business of my own invention. These are all accepted forms of married love, practiced by our venerable ancestors. The text and pictures prove it.'

Unsuspectingly, Noble Scent took the volume and opened it. When she turned to the second page and read the big bold heading: *Han-kung yi-chao*, 'traditional portraits from the imperial palace of the Han dynasty' (second century BC to second century AD), she thought, to herself:

'There were many noble and virtuous beauties at the court of the ancient Han rulers – the book must contain portraits of them. Very well, let us see what the venerable ladies looked like.' And eagerly she turned another page. But now came a picture that made her start back in consternation: in the midst of an artificial rock garden a man and woman in rosy nakedness, most intimately intertwined. Blushing crimson for shame and indignation, she cried out:

'Foo! How disgusting! Where did you ever get such a thing? Why, it sullies and befouls the atmosphere of my chaste bedchamber.'

Whereupon she called her maid and ordered her to burn the horrid thing on the spot. But he restrained her.

'You can't do that. The book is an ancient treasure, worth at least a hundred silver pieces. I borrowed it from a friend. If you wish to pay him a hundred silver pieces in damages, very well, burn it. If not, do me the favor of letting me keep it for two days until I have finished reading it; then I'll return it to my friend.'

'But why do you have to read such a thing, that offends against all human morality and order?'

'I beg your pardon, if it were as offensive and immoral as

all that, a famous painter would hardly have lent himself to illustrating it, and a publisher would hardly have been willing to defray the production costs and distribute the book. You are quite mistaken. Since the world was created, there has been nothing more natural and reasonable than the activities described in this book. That is why a master of the word joined forces with a master of color to fashion the material into a true work of art. Without such books love between the sexes would gradually lose all charm and ardor; husband and wife would bore one another to tears. Gone would be the pleasure of begetting children, dull indifference would take root. It is not only for my own edification that I borrowed the book, but wittingly and I think wisely for yours as well, in the hope that it would prepare you for motherhood, that your womb would be blessed and you would present me with a little boy or a little girl.'

Noble Scent was not entirely convinced.

'I cannot quite believe that what the book represents is really compatible with morality and reason. If that were so, why did our forebears who created our social order not teach us to carry on openly, in broad daylight, before the eyes of strangers? Why do people do it like thieves in the night, shut away in their bedchambers? Doesn't that prove that the whole thing must be wrong and forbidden?'

The Before Midnight Scholar replied with a hearty laugh.

'What a comical way of looking at things! But far be it from me to find fault with my *niang-tzu*, my dear little woman, on that account. It's all the fault of the preposterous way your honorable father raised you, shutting you up in the house and cutting you off from the outside world, forbidding you to associate with young girls like yourself who could have enlightened you. Why, you've grown up like a hermit without the slightest knowledge of the world. Of course married couples conduct their business by day as well as night; everyone does. Just think for a moment: if it had never been done in the daylight with others looking on, how would an artist have found out about all the different positions shown in this book? How could he have depicted all these forms and variations of loving union so vividly that one look at his pictures is enough to put us into a fine state of excitement?'

'Yes, but what about my parents? Why didn't they do it in the daytime?'

'I beg your pardon. How do you know they didn't?'

'Why, I would surely have caught them at it. I am sixteen, after all, and all these years I never noticed a thing. Why, I never even heard a sound to suggest that . . .'

Again the Before Midnight Scholar had to laugh aloud:

'Ah, what a dear little silly you are! Such parental occupations are not intended for the eyes and ears of a child! But one of the maids is sure to have heard or seen something from time to time. Of course your parents would never have done anything within your sight or hearing; very wisely they did it behind closed doors, for fear that if a little girl like you were to notice anything, her mental health might be upset by all sorts of premature thoughts and daydreams.'

After a moment of silent reflection, Noble Scent said, as though to herself:

'That's true. I remember that they occasionally withdrew to their bedchamber in the daytime and bolted the door after them – can that be what they were doing? It's possible. But in broad daylight! To see each other stark naked! How can it be? They must have felt so ashamed.'

'I beg your pardon. For lovers to see each other naked in broad daylight, why, that's the whole charm of it; it gives ten times more pleasure than doing it in the dark.'

Noble Scent was half convinced. Despite the modest 'no' of her lips, she was almost willing. A slight flush came to her cheeks, revealing her mounting excitement and anticipation of things to come. This did not escape him, and in secret he thought: 'She is gradually becoming interested. No doubt about it, she would like to play. But her senses have barely begun to awaken. Her hunger and thirst for love are very new to her. If I start in too brusquely, she is very likely to suffer the fate of the glutton who gobbles up everything in sight without taking time to bite or chew. She would get little enjoyment from such indigestible fare. I'd better bide my time and let her dangle a while.'

He moved to a comfortable armchair and sat down. Drawing her to him by the sleeve, he made her sit on his lap. Then he took the picture book and leafed through it page by page and picture by picture.

Unlike other books of a similar kind, the book was so arranged that the front of each leaf bore a picture and the back the text that went with it. The text was in two sections. The first briefly explained the position represented; the second gave a critical estimate of the picture from the standpoint of its artistic value.

Before starting, the Before Midnight Scholar advised his pupil to examine each picture carefully for its spirit and meaning, for then it would provide an excellent model and example for future use. Then he read to her, sentence for sentence.

'Picture No. 1. The butterfly flutters about, searching for flowery scents.'

Accompanying text: 'She sits waiting with parted legs on a rock by the shore of a garden pond. He, first carefully feeling out the terrain, takes pains to insert his nephrite proboscis into the depths of her calyx. Because the battle has only begun and the region of bliss is still far off, both still show a relatively normal expression, their eyes are wide open . . .'

Noble Scent obediently studied the pictures and patiently listened to the commentary. But as he turned another page and began to show her Picture No. 6, she pushed the book away in visible agitation and stood up.

'Enough!' she cried. 'What's the good of all these pictures? They are just upsetting. You look at them by yourself. I'm going to bed.'

'Just a little patience, we'll run through the rest quickly. The best is still to come. Then we'll both go to bed.'

'As if there weren't time enough tomorrow for looking at books. For my part, I've had quite enough.'

He embraced her and closed her mouth with a kiss. And as he kissed her, he noticed something new. They had been married for a whole month. In all that time, she had held the gates of her teeth closed tight when he kissed her. His tongue had never succeeded in forcing or wriggling its way through the solid fence. Until today he had never made contact with her tongue; he hadn't so much as an idea what it was like. But now when he pressed his lips to hers – what a wonderful surprise! – the tip of his tongue encountered the tip of her tongue. For the first time she had opened up the gate.

'My heart, my liver!' he sighed with delight. 'At last! And now – why bother moving to the bed? This chair will do the trick, it will take the place of the rock by the pond, and we shall imitate the lovers in Picture No. 1. What do you say?'

Noble Scent with affected indignation:

'Impossible. It's not a fit occupation for human beings . . .'

'There you are perfectly right. It is an occupation and pastime more fit for the gods. Come, let us play at being gods.' So saying, he stretched out his hand and began to fiddle with the knot of her sash. And despite her grimace of disapproval, she cooperated, letting him draw her close and permitting him to strip off her undermost covering. As he did so, he made a discovery that fanned his excitement into a bright flame. Aha, he thought, just looking at those pictures has sprinkled her little meadow with the dew of desire. He undid himself and set her down in the chair in such a way that her legs hung over his shoulders. Cautiously he guided his bellwether through the gates of her pleasure house, and then began to remove the rest of her clothes.

Why only now? you will ask. Why did he begin at the bottom? Let me explain: this Before Midnight Scholar was an experienced old hand. He said to himself that if he tried to remove her upper garments first, she would feel ashamed and intimidated, her resistance would make things unnecessarily difficult. That is why he daringly aimed his first offensive at her most sensitive spot, figuring that once she surrendered there she would easily surrender on all other fronts. Herein his strategy was that of the commander who defeats an enemy army by taking its general prisoner. And the truth is that she now quite willingly let him undress her from head to foot – no, not quite – with the exception of a single article of apparel which he himself tactfully spared: her little silk stockings.

After their three-inch long (or short) 'golden lilies' have been bound up, our women customarily draw stockings over the bandages. Only then do their toes and ankles feel at ease. Otherwise their feet, like flowers without leaves, are unlovely to behold.

Now he too cast off his last coverings and flung himself into the fray with uplifted spear. Already his bellwether was in her pleasure house. Groping its way to left and right, slipping and sliding, it sought a passage to the secret chamber where the 'flower heart', the privy seal, lies hidden. She helped him in his search by propping up her hands on the arms of the chair and, in tune with his movements, lithely twisting and bending her middle parts toward him. Thus they carried on for a time, exactly in accordance with Figure 2 of their textbook.

Suddenly, way down deep, she had a strange feeling of a kind that was utterly new to her: it did not hurt, no, it was more like a sensation of itching or tickling, almost unendurable, and yet very very pleasant.

'Stop,' she cried, bewildered by the strangeness of the thing. 'That's enough for today. You are hurting me.' And she tried to wrest herself free.

Thoroughly experienced in these matters, he realized that he had touched her most intimate spot, her flower heart. Considerately acceding to her wishes, he moved away from the ticklish spot and contented himself with moving his bellwether slowly back and forth several dozen times through her pleasure house with its narrow passages and spacious halls. The intruder made himself thoroughly at home on her property, and she was overcome by an irresistible desire to punish him for his insolence. Choking would be a fair punishment she thought.

Removing her hands from the arms of the chair, she let his back slip down and dug her hands into his buttocks. This enabled her to press closer to him, an operation in which he helped by clasping her slender waist in his hands and holding her as tightly as he could. Thanks to the intimate conjunction thus achieved – they were now exactly in the position illustrated in Figure 3 – she held his stiff thick bellwether firmly enough to start slowly strangling it. While sparing no effort and answering pressure with pressure, he saw that her eyes were clouding over and the stately edifice of her hair was becoming undone.

'*Hsin-kan*, my heart, my liver,' he panted. 'You seem to be on the verge – but it is very uncomfortable in this chair; shall we not continue on the bed?'

This suggestion did not appeal to her. She had the rascally intruder just where she wanted him; just a little longer, and she would choke the life out of him. At this late stage, she was quite unwilling to be cheated of her pleasure. If they were to move to the bed now, he would slip away from her. No, this was no time for interruptions! She shook her head resolutely. Then closing her eyes as though she were already half asleep, she said – this was her pretext – that she was much too tired to move.

He decided on a compromise: leaving her position unchanged, he placed his hands beneath her seat in such a way that she could not slip down, bade her throw her arms round his neck. Pressing his mouth to hers, he lifted her up carefully and thus enlaced carried her into the bedroom where they went on with the game.

Suddenly she let out a scream: 'Dearest, ah! ah!'

She pressed closer and closer to him and the sounds that

issued from her mouth were like the moans and groans of one dying. It was clear to him that she was on the threshold. And he too at the same time! With his last strength he pressed his nephrite proboscis into the sanctum of her flower-temple. Then for a time they lay enlaced as though in a deathlike sleep. She was first to stir; she heaved a deep sigh and said: 'Did you notice? I was dead just now.'

'Of course I noticed. But we don't call it "death". We call it "giving off an extract".'

'What do you mean by "giving off an extract"?'

'Both in man and woman a subtle essence of all the bodily humors is at all times secreted. At the peak of amorous pleasure one of the body's vessels overflows and gives off some of this extract. Just before the flow, the whole body, skin and flesh and bones, falls into a deep, unconscious sleep. Our physical state before, during, and after the flow is called *tiu* "a giving off of extract". It is depicted in Figure 5.'

'Then I was not dead?'

'Of course not. You gave off an extract.'

'If that is so, I hope I may do it day after day and night after night.'

He burst into a resounding laugh.

'Well, was I not right to recommend the picture book as an adviser? Is it not priceless?'

'Yes, indeed. A priceless treasure. We must consult it over and over again. A pity that the friend you borrowed it from will want it back again.'

'Don't you worry about that. It was I myself who bought it. The whole story about the friend was just made up.'

'Oh, that is good news.'

From then on the two of them were one heart and one

soul. Noble Scent became an assiduous reader of *The Vernal Palace* and from that day on she could not praise it too highly. Like a diligent pupil, she made every effort to put her learning into practice, and never grew weary of experimenting with the new forms and variations of the wind-and-moon game. The prim 'little saint' grew to be a past mistress at the arts of love. Determined to keep her vernal fires supplied with fuel, the Before Midnight Scholar ran untiringly from bookshop to bookshop, buying more books of the same kind, such as the *Hsiu-t'a yeh-shih*, 'The Fantastic Tale of the Silk-Embroidered Pillows', or the *Ju-yi-ch'ün chuan*, 'The Tale of the Perfect Gallant', or the *Ch'i p'o-tzu chuan*, 'The Tale of the Love-Maddened Women', and so on. In all he bought some twenty such books and piled them up on his desk.

Together they devoured each of the new acquisitions then put it away in the bookcase to make place for new reading matter. Both of them were so insatiable in their thirst for discovery that three hundred and sixty pictures of vernal positions could not have stilled their appetite. They were like the lovers we encounter in novels: an orchestra of lutes and guitars, a whole concert of bells and drums would not have sufficed to express the harmony and happiness in their hearts.

The Arousal of Inanna

Inanna's frank enjoyment of nascent desire and her vulva as one of its sources were a definite part of my inspiration for this book. Sumeriologists say that the word 'vulva', freely used once, has positive value. I regret its loss of respect and common currency today.

The maiden Inanna was present at the inundation.
From there she saved a tree
and planted it where she could tend it
and when it grew she awaited her reward
for this had been an act of worship.
She knew her destiny was to be Queen of Heaven.
She knew her body had begun to long for love
and as she waited she asked:

How long before I sit upon a radiant throne?
How long before I lie upon a radiant bed?

The goddess delighted in herself
Leaning against an apple tree
She observed her exquisite vulva
Enraptured by her exquisite vulva
She, the maiden, delighted herself

*Her companions joined her
as she celebrated herself*

I'll find a bridegroom,
let us dance, let us dance.
I will revel in my exquisite vulva,
let us dance, let us dance,
until he takes delight in it.

My vulva, the blessed vessel of the full moon,
the comely horn of the new moon,
an uncultivated field, growing wild, a grazing-
    meadow
rain-fed, curvaceous, enclosed.

For me, fertilize my vulva.
For the virgin land, who will be the cultivator?
For my vulva, moist and expectant,
who will provide the bull?
Plough my vulva, my chosen beloved.

My vulva is moist
I, the holy maiden Inanna, say my vulva is moist
Let my Chosen Lover place his hand on my vulva

You need not dig a channel, I will be your channel
You need not till a field; I will be your field
Farmer, do not look for moist ground
My sweet Love let me be your moist ground

I am chaste.
My nakedness is chaste.
It is fit for princes and gods
looking to tame wild kingdoms,
looking for land to prosper their realms.
I choose Dumuzi to be god of my land.

Inanna's mother heard about her song of desire,
Her brother and her father heard about her song of desire,
and they arranged the marriage of Inanna to Dumuzi.
But before they could break the news to her
She encountered Dumuzi in the city
And he pursued her to her door.
As Inanna walked home with her friends

Without my mother's permission
he's followed us
into the street where I live.
The young stallion
has pursued me here.
You've followed me here without permission

My father will be your father soon.
My mother will be your mother, too.
Let us discuss this.

And, your father will be my father,
your mother, my mother, too
Why not let me tell you all?

Inanna's friends cheered.
They are absorbed in delectable discussions, now,
delectable to the soul of those who want to argue:

With his jewels, Dumuzi
wants to lay the foundations of a house!

If only his small gems were for us to ornament our
　　necks.
If only his large jewels were for our virginal breasts!

Inanna looked over the balcony.
She stretched out towards him
and called out to Dumuzi, the wild bull:
Who are you building a house for?
With your gems?

I am building it for the hallowed one,
for my wife, the only one.
It's for her I'm building it.

Inanna, the holy maiden, is in love.
All she wants is to see Dumuzi again.
So when she sees his sister she speaks to her
And Geshtinanna takes her message to her brother.

I was walking past Inanna's house
when she saw me.
What did she tell me, Brother Dumuzi?
What did she speak of?

She spoke of her passion, your seductiveness, of
    her ecstasy.
She revealed to me
she had met you, dear brother,
she told me she had fallen in love with you
and she revels in fantasies of you.

I must go to her, sister,
I must go, Dumuzi cries.
Please, sweet Sister, let me go to her

High born and well brought-up,
I've eked out the time since yesterday.
I've tried to beguile time, by dancing,
by singing merry tunes from dawn to dusk,

And here he is! Here he is!
My beloved clasps my hand.
My beloved embraces me.

Let go of my hand, Shepherd! Let go of me!
I must go home.
Or how will I explain to my mother?
How can I deceive her?
I'll instruct you, Inanna,
I'll instruct you in the guile of maidens.

Say: 'My friend and I were walking
in the market.
Street musicians were playing their instruments.

We danced together,
we sang songs, sad and beautiful,
we sang songs, happy and beautiful.
Tell your mother a tale like that
so that we can be together
in the light of the moon.
I'll make you a bed fit for your prince.
I'll liberate your hair of its combs,
I'll pass rapturous moments with you,
in pleasure and harmony.

I'm no street wench, Inanna retorted.
I'll not embrace you or lie with you here.
I must return to my mother's house.

Dumuzi does not wish to offend Inanna.
He agrees to woo her honourably.

My lord wishes to call on my mother.
I am full of joy.
I wish I could alert my mother,
so that she can perfume the cedarwood floor!
Her house is scented and sweet-smelling
She will welcome him in joyfully.
Shepherd, I deem you worthy
Of the chaste embrace.
Dumuzi, you are gracious and worthy.
All your gifts are gracious and fragrant.

Then Inanna's brother Utu came to tell his maiden sister
that her wedding bed was to be prepared.

My sister, a bridegroom will lie beside you on
    the sheets.
Beside you will recline the equal of the Sky God.
Beside you will recline the son
of a hallowed womb.
Beside you will recline a man
brought forth to sit on a throne.

Can he be the man of my heart?
He is the man of my heart.
The man my heart knows.
Not a farmer, piling up his yield
But a shepherd who rears sheep, rich and fleecy.

On the day of the wedding, Utu comes to visit his sister,
    the bride Inanna.

My sister, have you prepared for the wedding?
Little one, have you prepared for the wedding?

I laved myself in water,
smoothed my skin with soap,
laved myself in water,
from a pitcher of burnished copper,
smoothed my skin with soap,
from a jar of polished stone.
I perfumed myself
With fragrant oil from a stone jar,
And robed myself in the gown of sovereignty,
The gown of heavenly sovereignty.

I smoothed my hair,
Which was tangled.
I dressed my locks,
which had strayed.
I combed them
and allowed them to trail
Down my shoulders
and my neck.
With golden rings
I ornamented my fingers.
Pretty precious beads
I draped around my throat,
ordered them carefully
and fastened them
with a gold cord.
Its jewelled tassel hangs down my back.

Inanna, I sought a good husband to delight your heart
Your tender heart, I sought to delight
Your patron goddess
has blessed you.
You bloom like the harvest.
You are luminous, like the honey-gold
mother who gave you birth.
My tender one, you are worth five of me.
My tender one, you are worth ten of me.
The goddess has moulded you,
created you flawless,
so Dumuzi longs to come
to my incomparable
and resplendent sister.

Fetch my bridegroom to me
From his mansion.
Send a man there
with a song of invitation.
Let me start to pour wine for my bridegroom.
Thus may his heart rejoice.
Thus may his heart be pleased.
Let him come, let him come!

My sister, let me lead you
to your bridal bed.
May your lover come to you like a lamb to the ewe.
O may he come.
My sister, let me lead you.

The shepherd's friends are generous and thriving.
The bridegroom's party are generous.
Your shepherd is their leader.
The farmer is his second.
The fowler is his third.
The fisherman, lord of the reed-beds
Is his fourth.

The bridal party put aside their work
To celebrate Inanna's wedding day.
They bring her the best of their produce.
The shepherd comes, weighed down
with gifts of creamy butter.
He brings urns of milk
and cheeses draped around his neck,
carrying delicately flavoured pails of milk

balanced on his shoulders.
He calls at Inanna's house.

Quickly now, open the door, queen of my heart!
quickly now open the door.

Chaste Inanna pauses
She listens to her mother's advice.

You are his wife, he is your husband.
He is for you, you are for him.
From now on your father is a stranger.
From now on your mother is a stranger.
Honour his mother as your own.
Honour his father as your own.

Dumuzi calls: Open the door, queen of my heart!
Quickly, now, open the door.

Inanna, prepared as her mother had advised,
washed in fresh water and laved in scented oils,
dressed in her regal robes,
smoothes in place her breast amulets,
arranges again her necklace of lapis lazuli,
stands waiting,
holding her seal of sovereignty.
Dumuzi strikes the door,
and like moon-water she flows towards him
from her house.
He gazes at her, exults in her.
He grasps her in his arms and kisses her.

Dumuzi takes Inanna to the chapel of his patron
   god.

O Inanna, I bring you to the chapel of my god,
you will sit in grace on his seat.
Though he honoured her in this way,
Inanna sat beneath the dais saying:
You must guide me. I always did my mother's
   bidding.

Dumuzi holds Inanna close.
I will not make a slave of you.
You will eat at a grand table.
Oh, my bride, you will not weave for me.
Oh, Inanna, you will not spin for me.
Oh, my bride, you will not ravel my fleece for me.

Inanna turns and embraces Dumuzi.
I, the luminous goddess shine golden in the dawn
   sky.
Dumuzi, my shepherd, I who am numinous,
   shine golden in the dusk sky,
I gleam golden for you.

Dumuzi is dazzled by Inanna and praises her.

The Sacred queen on high
I salute
the heavenly queen
Inanna.
I salute

the dazzling flare of the firmament
the heavenly night-glow, illuminating as daylight
the heavenly Queen.
I salute you.

Holy and awesome Queen,
purest of the pure,
wearing the crown of two horns,
first child of the Divine Moon,
Inanna, I salute you.

Her splendour and her might,
her high birth,
her dazzling appearance,
in the dusk sky
like a flaming brand,
her ascent in the night sky
like the moon,
in the dawn sky,
like the sun
adored by all the world,
these are the words of my song.

Dumuzi, you must swear to me
that no rival of mine
has kissed your lips
before I discard
my splendid gown, gossamer fine,
and reveal my nakedness to you.
My beloved, who beguiles and enchants me
I demand a pledge from you.

Oh, beautiful man,
place your right hand
on my vulva.
Cradle my head with your left hand
as your mouth draws close to mine
and you enclose my lips and yours.
Pledge me your loyalty.

Oh, my flowering one,
how you delight me!
My garden of apple-blossom,
how you delight me!
My immaculate column,
how you delight me!
My marble column studded with lapis lazuli,
you delight me!

Man of my heart, my dear one,
let's make your delightful gifts,
glorious honey,
choicer still.

My beloved, my commander,
who advances towards me,
I retreat from you
to my bed.

I long for you
to play tender games with me.
My own beloved,
cover me in your honey sweetness.

In the golden honey corner of the bridal room
we'll delight, again and again
in your glorious honey.
I long for you
to play tender games,
my own beloved,
games that lave me in your honey sweetness.

When you first loved me
I wished that I could let you play
sweet games with me.

There, where you could pour
your sweetness into me
honey-sweet
pour in your tenderness
please, fill it there for me
like barley in a bushel.

O pound it there for me
Like barley in a bushel.

Strongly, he bloomed,
strongly, he bloomed and bloomed,
and watered my lettuce field.
From his black, fertile wild grass
did my beloved
water my barley stalk in its voluptuous groove.
He watered my lettuce,
my dear one, an apple tree burdened at the top with fruit,
watered my garden!

O my lover, who all at once pleasurably
filled me inside to the navel.
My wilderness, honey loins
you fertilised, my lettuce mound.

Oh, my splendid-haired love,
luscious and sturdy
as a date palm,
my lover who kisses my breast to greet me,
honoured in the assembly . . .

You are my crown jewel,
the gold I wear,
my amulet carved by
an ingenious artisan.

My cherished bride exalts me far and wide
Her praise sugared like her vulva
Her vulva sugared like her praise.

My plumage, like foliage, he'll water
and stroke the fledgling in its nest.
My maid has tended my feathers,
arranged them in an elegant crest,
has lovingly groomed it
and is arraying my breast with jewels
Let him nestle in my petals,
delectable foliage.
Arouse Dumuzi, make him ready
to fulfil his passion.

May my attractions be unsurpassable to him,
may he enchant me for ever.

You are truly our lord,
silver wrought with lapis lazuli.
You are truly our farmer bringing in much grain.

The fruit of my eye, the longing of my heart,
may you see many dawns
may you have a long life!

SECTION TWO

Desire

The Tobacco Plant
North American-Indian

Izanagi and Izanami
Ancient Japanese

The Queen of the Summer Country
Medieval English

Eset's Love Quest
Ancient Egyptian

The Ballad of Skirnir
Medieval Icelandic

The Tobacco Plant

I wish there had been more of this sweet story, which says simply that love makes the world go round. In this tiny fragment the 'gaze of desire' works its wondrous magic.

A young man and a girl travelled together, fell in love and left the path for the happiness of intercourse. They were so pleased that they agreed to marry. Later, on a hunting journey, the man returned to the place where they had first united and there found a pretty flower with scented leaves. He took it back to the people and told of the discovery. They said, 'When it is dried, we will smoke it, and name it "Where We Came Together".' The elders of the tribes claimed that because the man and woman were so completely at peace and happy when tobacco was made it has been smoked ever since at councils for promoting peace and friendship between the tribes.

Izanagi and Izanami

This story is a Japanese account of desire and the first act of love between the progenitors of humankind. This is where it all began.

The gods looked down from the heavens and spoke to Izanagi the god and Izanami the goddess as they stood on the Floating Bridge of Heaven.

'There is a land near you. It is low and flat and lush with reed-beds and able to produce a rich and abundant harvest. It is your duty to create order in it.'

To help them do this, they reached down and gave the divine couple the jewel-spear of the heavens. Izanagi and Izanami took the spear and probed the waters, swirling it deep and wide, looking for a piece of land. When they found none, they withdrew the spear from the waters. As it hung above the waters, the ocean foam sprayed from its blade, fanning out, spreading and crystallizing until it formed an island.

'We will call the island Ono-goro-jima,' decided Izanagi and Izanami. So saying, they floated down from the bridge and went to the island, which they made their home. They took the jewel-spear of heaven and planted it in the earth as

they would one day plant the fields. And around it they con-
structed the palace in which they would live. This palace
was so large that they called it the Eight Fathom Palace.
Izanami and Izanagi wished to remain connected with
heaven and the other gods so they created a vast pillar,
which joined their land to heaven.

Order was emerging in their world and they were achieving it together. They looked at each other and sighed. There
was a feeling within them that neither had experienced
before and they were not sure what to do about it, how to
express it. But every day, as they set about their tasks, the
feeling became more intense. Izanami felt the surge of emotion in her companion's presence; she felt a tingling on her
skin when they came close. When they touched she felt a
dart of fire heat the centre of her body – a flame active in her
source that told her she was a woman. Did Izanagi feel it
too? Izanami had to know: she could no longer hold back.

So the next time she saw him, she cried, 'How beautiful!
A fine young man.'

Izanagi was shocked that the goddess had made such a
bold statement. It was not appropriate. He, the man, should
have made the first move. 'We must return to heaven,' he
said, 'and tell the gods exactly what has happened.'

So the divine pair climbed the great pole to heaven and
told the gods their story. The gods listened quietly then gave
their advice.

'Since the woman spoke before the man and reversed the
correct order, you must stay here in heaven for a time. Then
you may return and begin again.' The second time they took
no chances.

✳

Izanagi, the male, approached the pillar from the left, the superior direction, while Izanami, the female, approached from the right in keeping with protocol. Slowly they moved towards each other. Excitement filled both of them. They overflowed with delight and desire as they came near.

This time Izanagi wasted no time. 'How beautiful! An enchanting woman.'

They drew close and embraced. They explored each other, touching, kissing, enjoying each other's bodies. But there was something else. Something remaining. The more they embraced and kissed, the more impassioned they became, the greater their desire. Izanagi felt the flame fiery in his loins, the sap surging in his member and longed to know if Izanami knew the same pleasurable pain.

'Is there any part of you that has a will of its own?' he asked.

'There is a part of me that has a will of its own. It is my woman part.'

'I, too, have a part with a will of its own. It is my man part. And I long to merge mine with yours.'

They clung to each other, unwilling to let go, but still unsure what to do next. Their male and female parts touched and caressed and enlarged and moistened but instead of feeling fulfilled, their desire was inflamed even further. Then they sensed another presence. They saw two birds with long tails. Intrigued, they watched as the birds hopped about for an instant, before one approached the other and mounted it, moving upwards and downwards, back and forth, in a wonderful, rhythmic movement. Izanagi and Izanami gazed, hypnotized, their eyes following the movements of the birds' tails and heads, swaying in harmony.

Slowly, almost unconsciously, Izanami and Izanagi began to emulate the actions of the birds, swaying in unison, in concord with each other. His manhood and her womanhood came together, their bodies fused and finally they achieved their rapture.

They were now husband and wife and gave birth to many children.

The Queen of the Summer Country

Did Lancelot and Guenevere make love at the Castle of Dolorous Garde? The question is much debated. Chrétien never revealed whether participants of amor cortois *refrained from carnal relations. This is Rosalind Miles's view.*

'Leave me, Ina.'

Ina pursed her lips and slipped quietly away. Goddess, Mother, she wondered, what's wrong with the Queen? Surely she could not be so distressed about her knights? Sir Bors had a fever, it was true, but he was young and healthy, he would shake it off. The others were recovering well from the cuts and blows they had taken in the wood. And Sir Lancelot had arrived to rescue them all!

Yet the Queen . . . Watching Guenevere covertly as she turned down the sheets of the lavender-scented bed, Ina could not make it out. After all they had been through, to be crying, shaking, weeping now? From the trembling in her hands, you'd have thought she had a fever, yet she would not countenance any of Ina's potions or soothing balms.

'Leave me, Ina,' was all that she would say.

Ina snorted quietly to herself. Leave her here, by the window, in the cold light of the moon, all weeping and alone? The Queen her mother would never have wanted this. Ina gathered her strength to remonstrate. 'My lady,' she began forcefully.

Guenevere's voice was as distant as the moon. 'Leave me, Ina. I'll call you when I want you. Leave me now.'

You must leave me.

She had hurt Ina, she knew, with her sharp rebuff. But she could not help it. She could not help anything now.

For now she felt the force of Merlin's curse, when Arthur had fought Malgaunt to the death. 'If you spare this man,' Merlin had told Arthur, then 'you will suffer for it all your living days. Malgaunt is fated to destroy your peace. He will rob you of your best jewel, and leave a gaudy imitation in its place. All this he will do because you spared his life.'

She had sought to avoid her kinsman's blood on her marriage bed. She wanted to spare Arthur from it as much as Malgaunt, and turn evil to good to bless their wedding day. But Malgaunt's malice had already woven its web. Arthur's peace was destroyed when Malgaunt's actions brought Lancelot here.

She had fled like a child from the fear of Lancelot's love. But the force of fate had drawn him here, and her love for Arthur lay in ruins now.

Her love had been the jewel in Arthur's crown. And what was left but imitation now?

Alone in the bedchamber, Guenevere sat in the window in grief too deep for tears. He had come for her, Lancelot, her lord, her hope, her love. He had come like the celandines in springtime, like the first soft fall of the snow. And she had lied to him, and sent him away.

To save his life?

But did he know that? Would he ever know?

So again he had offered his service, and his trust had been abused. Would he ever trust her simplest word again? Why should he? Would she, in his place?

She rose to her feet, gripped the iron bars of the deep, mullioned window, and pressed her burning head against the glass. Below her the garden was drowsing as night fell. The scent of the roses was heavier in the evening air, and the warmth of day was leaving the old stone walls. The candle-light from her window cast its lambent glow into the deepening dark. All the world below her was at peace.

The iron bars were cold and rough in her grasp. She groaned. She was still a prisoner, even though Malgaunt had drawn off his watchdogs now that Lancelot was here. Yet this barred room was a place of safety, and she had been glad to take refuge here from the courtyard, refusing to join Malgaunt and Lancelot at dinner in the hall.

But there was no escaping from herself. From this love, this shame, this sickness that she had.

She moaned aloud.

Her only hope was that he did not know.

His head pounding, Lancelot stumbled out of doors. Dolorous Garde! The place was well named.

To come to the aid of the Queen in her distress, and then to find she was not in distress at all – to be treated to a smiling rebuke that was worse than any scorn and then to have to drink and dine with her kinsman, that foul slave Malgaunt. Goddess, Mother, this was not the life of chivalry he had dreamed of!

He lifted his face to the moon, letting the cool night air bathe his tormented skin. When he served Queen Aife, she held all her knights in thrall. She was a stern task-mistress, and her knights groaned in her service, she demanded so much of them. But never did they suffer in confusion like this.

A gasp that was half a sob escaped his lips as he wandered on through the castle grounds. He passed under archways and through gates till he came to a quiet garden enclosed within old stone walls. In the centre a great hawthorn sprinkled the grass with stars. He let himself in through the small iron gate and felt safe and alone at last.

From the walls, the scent of June roses drenched the air. High above, the uncaring stars looked down. He tore a rose from a stem and crushed it in his hand. The sharp sweetness of the broken petals stained his clenched fist. He lifted his eyes to the stars, opened his heart, and wept.

She saw him coming, it seemed, from the time before time. First a shadowy figure in the gold and silver light, then the lean shape she loved so desperately. Then the swing of his cloak, the glint of the torque round his neck. And then the dull chestnut sheen of his hair and his long, tormented face. And now he stood in the garden beneath her window, his eyes bright with tears, waiting, she was sure, for her call.

Yet he stood in a silence she did not know how to break. The blood was pounding in her veins, and foolish thoughts ran through her mind. *If only there were someone else here to call him instead of me.*

Wildly she fingered the woodland green silk gown she had not changed since she was captured. *If only I'd worn something better, if only I'd known he was on his way!* Yet would he notice what she was wearing? Would he care?

She lifted her eyes to the distant sky. Far away on the horizon a horned moon was shining and all the heavens were burning with pale fire.

Come —

From the airy mansions of the moon, and the far regions of the world between worlds, he was calling her. She could hear the soft insistent whisper of life itself.

Come —

She opened the window and whispered, 'Lancelot!'

He started like a stag, his hand unconsciously seeking his sword. Then he stepped into the light from the window, looking up as pale and cold as stone. 'Why did you go?' he began abruptly, staring at her with the hurt eyes of a child. 'I am your knight. Why did you send me away? Why did you leave Caerleon without a word?'

'I thought —'

He turned on her in a rage. 'Why did you lie to me? Lie and deceive?' He flew at the wall, and tore at the ivy in despair.

'I —'

He was climbing now, surging up the massive old creeper with a fearless grip. 'You sent me to the King with a message that was no message at all! You left orders that I was to stay in Caerleon till you returned. You wanted to be parted from me while you were away! Why? Do you have a lover? Another knight?'

Her temper rose to match his. 'If you are my knight, sworn to my love and faith,' she cried, possessed by wild illogic, 'why are you here when I ordered you to stay?'

He had reached the window-ledge, almost within her touch, borne up by desire and pain. 'Because I thought you were in danger – because I had to know what you meant – because I could not bear it without you!'

'Oh, Lancelot—'

He was weeping freely, angrily knocking away great tears. 'You may treat your knight badly, but I am still sworn to you. Wherever you go, I must go!' He reached towards her blindly, like a motherless child.

She could feel her tears rising in answer to his. 'How did you find me?'

He planted his feet in the ivy and gripped the iron bars with both hands. She could hardly bear his open, wounded gaze. 'Lady, I would have found you in all the world! When I came to Camelot, they said you were lost in the wood. They told me no one was more distraught than Prince Malgaunt. Yet I knew the Prince was next in line for your throne. And when they said he had a castle beyond the forest, I knew where to come. I knew I would find you here.'

'You knew? How?' She leaned on the window-sill. His nearness tormented her.

He shook his head stubbornly, like a child again. 'I knew.' He raised his eyes and locked on to her gaze. She knew she was looking into his soul. His purple-brown irises were flecked with hazel and gold, and his face was wet with tears. She lifted her hand to his lips as she had on the night they met, and let it fall again.

The air was warm, and the tension between them was a thread about to break. His eyes were wide with query, and she answered without words. Furiously he pulled at the bars of the window, till he found one set less firmly than the others in the stone. Then he worked at it steadily, twisting it this way and that, till his forehead was damp with sweat, and the iron was dark with what looked like his blood.

She wanted to laugh, to cry, to dance.

So this is love – welcome, friend, as cruel as you will be, and as sweet as you may become.

Welcome love.

May we be granted the peace of loving and not losing, of giving and not resenting, may we let this newborn thing grow and florish between us, and become what it has to be.

Now she could feel herself growing into the woman she had dreamed she might become, moving towards the man who was all she wanted in a man. She could hear his breath rasping in his throat as he wrenched the bar out of its mortar at last. He groaned with the exertion, and she could see the rusty metal had torn the skin of his palms. The veins on his forehead were standing out, and his eyes had an Otherworldly gleam, but no man could have looked more beautiful to her now.

He heaved himself up, and was through the remaining bars, over the casement and into the room in one sinuous move. As he came towards her she saw that his hands were red with blood.

She ran towards him, and reached up to touch his face. The skin of his temple was damp to her fingertips. The hollow by his eyes seemed to have been waiting for her caress, and she wanted to trace the shape of his cheekbones till the day she died.

Her hand found the back of his neck, and he shuddered, but did not pull back. Gently, slowly, she drew his face down to hers, and laid her finger in the groove of his lips. He seized her hand, and pressed it to his mouth Then he grasped her like a man starving, folded her in his arms and kissed her for the first time.

Outside the window the moon shone down on groves of white hawthorn and roses with silver leaves, making their branches sing. The pale fragrance of apple blossom was in the air. She kissed his mouth hungrily, and felt his hunger rise. She kissed him again, she was starving for him – *oh, my love, my love*.

He gasped and stepped back, only to crush her to him tighter than before. 'The glory of the spring shines in you alone, and the splendour of the stars lives in your eyes!' he moaned. 'You are the woman of the dream, you are the love I have longed for all my life. But you are married, you are the wife of the King! Oh, lady, lady, what does it mean?'

'Hush,' she said. 'Hush, my love.'

She kissed the welling blood from his hand and drew him towards the bed.

They stood by the bed and kissed like people famished for each other since time began. His kisses were hard and hungry like a boy's, and she could feel his passion building with every breath. Trembling, she took his face between her hands. The soft stubble of his chin pricked her fingers, but the skin was as smooth as satin on his temples, and in the tender hollow of his throat.

She wanted to weep as she threaded her fingers through his hair. The back of his neck was as soft as down, and he trembled at her touch. She wrapped her arms round him, and he clasped her to him so fiercely that he lifted her off her feet. 'Ah, lady!' he whispered. 'Is this a dream?'

Sighing, he buried his face in her neck. His lips made a path of kisses round her throat. Inside her gown her skin was pricking for his touch. He brought his hand to her breast, and her body caught fire.

She reached up to her headdress, and cast the golden circlet and veil to the ground. As she raised her face to his, her hair fell down like rain. Gasping, he explored her mouth and she savoured his long full lips, his strong, insistent tongue. Then he lifted her, and swung her on to the bed.

Kneeling astride, deftly he untied the fastenings of her gown. A blistering shaft of remembrance shot through her mind: *Arthur fumbled my buttons the first time he came to me*. Then he pushed back the green silk to her navel, till she was as naked as a lily in its sheath of leaves. She lifted her arms to his neck, her eyes met his gaze, and she thought of Arthur no more.

As the gown slipped down and she lay bare to him, Lancelot made a soundless cry in the back of his throat. His eyes grew bright with tears. Her breasts were white and full, her nipples rosy and sweet as kisses in the night, and already craving his touch. In her body, in her eyes, in every distracted movement and light moan, he could feel her love and need calling out to his own. The sound of his own name dimly reached his ears. She was crooning it almost to herself, lifting her arms to him, wrapping them round his neck.

She was aching for him now, crying out under her breath. He reached out in wonder and stroked the top of her breasts. Her nipples tensed in answer to his caress. She reached for his fingers and crushed them against her breast till she groaned in pain. Then she drew him down beside her on the bed, and took him in her arms.

Gently she stroked his back, his sides, and the lean, tense curve of his flanks. Then her hand found the opening of his shirt and her fingers brushed his breast. He started violently, leaped to his feet and, unbuckling his heavy leather belt, tore off his tunic and shirt, and kicked off his breeches and boots.

Naked, he was white and golden like a god. A silver dewdrop glinted on the top of his sex. Gilded by the gold and silver dusk, he was a being from the Otherworld. He leaned over, and peeled away the last remnant of her modesty, drawing the green gown down over her hips. Then he slipped down beside her on the bed, and dropped a rainfall of sweet kisses on her quivering flesh.

The touch of his lips felt like the sun in spring, after the longest winter she had known. Tenderly he explored the dewy triangle at the top of her legs till she writhed under his hand. She felt herself grow wet with joy for him, and a mist of tears came before her eyes. She clung to him in a storm of emotion, of love, of fear, she could not tell. A thought of Arthur passed through her like a knife, and she caught her breath with pain. *What am I doing?* she moaned to herself. *Why am I here?* Then Lancelot renewed his caresses and she could think no more.

Now she was riding the waves of desire as they battered her senseless, pulling her down to the dark rolling depths. He quickened with her till she could not tell where his body ended and hers began. Now they were breathing the same panting breaths, and the need between them could not be contained. She opened her arms and cried out to him from her heart, *'Love me, Lancelot, love me, love me now!'*

And he cried out too, and came into her, and the roaring sea drowned them both.

Afterwards they drowsed in each other's arms. Lancelot held her close, but she could hear the doubt and wonder in his voice. 'When did you know?'

Lazily she traced the fine skin of his eyelids, the tender blue of harebells in spring. 'As soon as I saw your eyes.'

He paused. 'What, the very first time we met, in the forest? When I came with Bors and Lionel?'

'There. I could have lain down for you there.'

He was silent. Anxiety seared her like a flame. He could have had any girl, one of his own age who had never borne children, who did not have the telltale marks of motherhood. Perhaps he hated her body, now that they had made love. Perhaps he did not love her, he never had – She forced herself to speak. 'And you? When did you know?'

The silence lengthened and deepened till she could feel the ground shifting, and a chasm between them opening now. She clutched at him. 'You do know, don't you? Say you know!'

He opened his eyes. 'You knew,' he said gently, settling her back in his arms. 'That is enough.'

And she knew that it was not the last time she would feel that pain.

Eset's Love Quest

Eset epitomizes the infinite eroticism of longing for an absent lover. Her sexual union with Osiris symbolized the well-being of the world; her loss spelt its destruction and a period of drought and darkness.

She stands by the water's edge. Voices – soft ones, loud ones, happy and sad – float across her mind; dark, transparent clouds suspend her vision. Strands of her hair billow across her eyes, mixing with the clouds, her tears falling.

'Osiris! Where are you?' Her fingers twist into the nimbus of black around her head as a wail emanates from her depths. 'Where did you go?'

The women around her look down at her reflection, rising from the feet, elongating, expanding, widening – terrifying. All else is stillness. The reflection blurs, shatters. Eset beats her breast with one ivory hand, then the other.

'Why? Why?' she howls. 'Why did you listen to him? Why did you get into the sarcophagus? Why?'

Nephthys tugs at Eset's arms, restraining her. 'I was no part of it, sister. I hope you know.'

Eset is suddenly dull. 'It doesn't matter. Nothing matters.'

The life has gone from her voice. The vitality has gone

from the lustre of the leaves. The sun glows without warmth or brightness. Since Osiris went and left her grieving the birds have stopped singing. Eset mourns her loss silently now. She watches the hubris of Set as he robes himself in the garments of Osiris' splendour, dreaming of the crown and sceptre of kingship to replace her lover, his brother.

'She does nothing. She does nothing. She does nothing.' The whispered echo susurrates through the kingdom. 'Eset does nothing while Set prepares to take over Egypt.'

Eset raises her head. 'Who says I do nothing?' She rises from her position on the ground, smoothes her unkempt hair. 'I am leaving in search of Osiris. I cannot let him go so easily.'

There is a hole where her heart once was – but it is heavy with sickly vapour. Her breasts are like volcanoes, run with channels of blazing, melting lava. Her arms ache when she remembers she can no longer hold him. The only way she can survive the separation is to think of the happy times. Ah! What happy times they were.

- In embryo they were already entwined, twin souls. In the sky womb of Nut, arched over Geb's earth-form, Eset and Osiris lay side by side, holding each other. They moved enclosed in the star-filled waters, caressing finger-tip to fingertip, nuzzling nose to nose, brushing lips against lips. They were made for each other. Eset the leader, the active one, held him firmly as they emerged from starlight into earth-dawn. She watched her other half as he turned radiant, slowly illuminating heaven and earth with spreading, all-encompassing light.
- 'It's warm,' mused Eset, enclosing the air in her palms.

- Though he grew tall and majestic and lit up the cosmos with his brightness, Eset knew the soft vulnerability that filled her brother's soul, his being. In childhood, she became his guardian, protecting him from their sibling Set. And as the world began to teem with lesser beings, she guarded him. When Osiris assumed the role of teacher, wandering through the furthest corners of the world, spreading knowledge about the grain, bringing song to every human heart, it was she who drove off his foes. She was clever-tongued in his defence and her speech never failed to divert the deeds of the dissenters. But now she had failed him. Where had she been when Set finally succeeded in his mischief? One moment of distraction – and Osiris was gone.

The reverie breaks. Eset stands at the waterside, searching searching the river where Set's men had turned adrift the sarcophagus containing Osiris. How many days had it been? How far could it have drifted? Oh, Nile, oh Nile, have you protected or failed him? Should she follow on foot or on water? Eset puts her hands to her head, then starts to run to the palace, lamenting wildly. 'Come to your house, Osiris, your foes are not there. Oh, my beautiful musician, return to your palace.'

But Osiris does not appear, nor can she hear his voice.

In her chamber, she tears off her glorious robes, her jewels, her adornments, smears the antimony from her eyes, wipes away the redness from her lips. Naked, she takes a sharp knife and slashes away locks of her hair. Then she clothes herself in the starkness of mourning. Head high, she walks slowly, majestically, through the great hall of the palace without a glance at the throne that is her essence, the seat that held Osiris.

'Look at me, I'm your beloved, your sister. The Only One. Do not leave me. I mourn in my heart. I search with my eyes. Good King, won't you let me see you?'

Where is Osiris? Why does he not respond? Does he think she was angry with him? Her heart wrenches as she recalls their disagreement before he left to go to Set's banquet. Did he allow himself to be duped because he thought she would not have him back? She must find him to know the answers.

Without a backward inclination of her head, she's gone. She's left the palace. Her journey has begun.

'While I can see,' she vows, 'I'll call to you, weeping to the limit of the skies.'

So Eset becomes the Weeping Woman, travelling all the distances to the extremes of the lands that embrace the waters. Up the Nile, down the Nile, searching the caves, ferreting through the forests. Everywhere there are signs of Osiris. In the swaying wheat and corn, she sees his skills of husbandry. In the song-making and dancing of local festivities, she hears his voice, his words, his rhythms. But nowhere does she find him. Sometimes she can hear a sound, sense a movement, see a golden glow among the crowds, in the wildernesses, in temples, and her heart starts to thump. Osiris? But it is never Osiris, only a faithful worshipper.

Eset raises her head to the skies. Nut, her mother, smiles down at her in a spangle of stars. 'You remember, Eset?' she muses. 'You remember when he left you before to come to me and lay open his heart to you? He left you then, too. And you came to learn it was not a leaving. He always returned, always with a fuller heart than the one that set him on his path. You and Osiris, you are one soul. You can never be parted.'

The consolation is empty for Eset. She feels the nothingness around her. She needs touch, she needs vision, she needs sound. In this, her world of colour and fragrance, intangible essence means little. She has amends to make, questions to answer: an ethereal, intangible nearness of the senses is not enough. Nevertheless Nut's words make her smile.

- They ran through the reed thickets, the soles of their feet sparking fire on the sands, she running, he chasing, laughing, breathless, until her foot caught in a treacherous root lying concealed in the rippled layers of sand. In no time he was upon her.
- 'I've caught you now,' he exulted. She flailed, fending him off, as she screamed, laughing still, 'You're a cheat.'
- 'A cheat?' he growled. 'How's that?'
- 'I fell. It doesn't count if you fall.'
- 'Love has no protocol,' he retorted. 'There are no rules here.'
- Eset's movements stopped. She held his face in her hands, looking hard at it. He looked back into her eyes, his gaze intense, challenging until she could look no longer at the frankness of his desire and her eyes closed.
- 'Look at me, Eset,' Osiris commanded. 'Tell me what you see in my eyes.'
- Eset turned aside her face. The curve of her cheek screened her turmoil. She could feel his soft breath against it, on her neck, and she felt a warm fluid gush through her

body, like a wave. It made her tremble. In a flash she twisted her body beneath him, attempting to slip away. But he held fast.

- She clenched her lids tight. She knew her eyes were a mirror that would confirm his longing. Suddenly, she was shy as she had never before been with him. Something was changing. Something was different. If she gave in they would become different.

- 'Open your eyes.'

- Eset twisted again, and managed to slide away from under him. But as she stood, she stumbled with a cry: 'My ankle.'

- Osiris held her, gently pulling her down.

- 'Show me where it hurts.' He grasped her ankle firmly. 'It's slender and supple, like the stem of a lotus-blossom.'

- Eset smiled, laughter welling up on another gush of fluid warmth. She wanted to fling her arms around Osiris, to kiss his mouth and drink the sweet wine that she knew suddenly was in it. She looked into his face, engaged the same intent gaze. They must have sat that way for an aeon, eyes locked, experiencing the tremors and uncertainties of first love. Then Osiris swept her up in his arms and walked over to the water's edge. He set her down in the soft sand, then dug slowly until he had moulded a bed. There he placed her, trembling.

- Eset snuggled into the sandy hollow, feeling the warmth of the sun. The sands pressed in around her, and she closed her eyes.

- Osiris walked away. He was picking flowers. He returned, wove reed-braids for her hair, then gently lifted its strands to trail them across his face, his cheek, his neck, his breast, before winding them through the fresh green reeds. He gave her posies of riverside flowers. He smoothed away the golden glitter of sand from her neck, sliding his hands slowly up and down the fresh skin, moist with silt and desire. She felt her heart beat against him like drumbeats before a battle. Her vision was blurring. She saw him surrounded by dazzling light, as if each ray that touched his royal head was creating a new sun, just for him. Each stroke of his hand stoked a wavering fire inside her.

- What will I do? she thought wildly. What must I do? She lay very still, receptive, passive, as she felt his hands encircle the base of her throat like a necklace, her vision blazing blue like lapis beneath her sealed lids, edged with a fraying purple. His warm lips brushing her neck made her moan with pleasure. 'Osiris.'

- 'I'm here, my sweet, my sister. Just you and I together, always, made for each other.'

- Her arms rose, her hands clasped together around him.

- 'Made together,' she echoed, 'for each other, since the beginning of time.'

- Osiris retreated and her eyes flickered open. Where was he going? She saw him reach away, a flicker of panic running through her. Was he leaving her? Had she done something wrong? But then he placed tiny clusters of grapes on her breasts; they glistened, translucent purple, against the light. The vein of stems holding them together tapered up to a fine, perky point. Osiris' lips nipped and teased it. His short, sharp breath, falling on her breasts, seeped through the small, pointed mounds, sending fire through each vein. Slowly, patiently, he grasped each amethyst fruit in his mouth until they had all gone. His lips were on her skin now, the tip of his tongue drawing circles around the base of her breasts. How they filled and swelled. Eset squirmed, tense, expectant, until his mouth closed firmly around her nipple.

- 'Sweet wine,' he murmured. 'Sweeter than the grape.'
- She tried to speak but her voice was heavy and tremulous with intoxication. Her hips moved of their own accord and she averted her face hoping Osiris would not notice its stark desire as he rested his head on her breast and she clasped him there with both hands, stroking his face, burying her hands in his hair. She could feel his tongue, now, tracing a long line down before it rested on her softly rounded belly.
- What is happening to me? she thought, alarmed. What are we doing?
- She attempted to rise. Osiris sensed her concern, clasped her hands, his fingers interlacing with hers in a private dance, as he lowered his head further. With a startled cry, Eset pulled away. This fire would burn her. It would consume them both.
- Osiris looked up at her. The hurt in his eyes was deep.
- 'No!' she said.
- 'Why?'
- 'I don't know.'
- 'Then don't resist.'
- 'We must resist.'
- 'You are the throne, I am the king. Our union is inevitable.'
- Eset sat up. 'We must stop, Osiris.'
- 'Eset, this is our destiny,' he insisted. 'What shame can there be in our union?'

- 'Union?' she mused.
- 'We have always been inseparable, always loved like this.'
- 'Not like this,' she replied slowly. 'But, yes, we have always loved.'
- 'Then this is our fate, the next step to eternal union.'
- Eset's eyes filled with tears. 'Don't compel me, Osiris. You know I've never refused you anything. But this . . .'
- 'Why are you alarmed? We have always touched. We embraced in the womb.'
- Eset was seized with fear of losing him. For once in her life she was uncertain, unsure what to do. 'It was different.'
- Slowly, Osiris stood up. 'Then so be it.'
- Eset reached out, grasped his hand. 'Where are you going?'
- 'I can't be with you as before, Eset, but I will never force you.'
- She clung to his arm, shivering. For a moment he looked as if he would give in, come back to her, caress her, kiss her, comfort her. But, with a wrenching movement, he shook off her hand.
- Eset watched, dazed, tears spilling. She had resisted too far. Now she had lost him.
- 'Osiris!' she called. 'Come back.'
  Osiris walked slowly to the water's edge and leapt into a skiff moored to a tree stump.
- 'Where are you going, Osiris?'
  He did not reply.
  'Osiris! Come back. Don't leave me. We must be together.'
- Osiris' eyes were filled with sadness as he looked at her a last time. She could see the determination glint, steely, beneath the grief.

- 'Not as before, Eset. Never again as before.'
- Eset's heart stood still. This was what she had feared. She was different inside, hollow. If he stayed she would do as he asked – she, too, desired it with all her body and soul. But she would not call him back with that promise. If he wanted to return to her, he had to come for her sake.
- She turned and walked home. From her door, she looked back. Her gaze flew to the remote end of her street. There was no sign of Osiris. She had hurt him and he was gone. Eyes streaming, she pulled the door of her mansion violently shut and dashed her weight against the great bolts, so that they rattled and clattered as she locked them. If Osiris would not visit her, no one could. Her doors would be locked. On the other side, somewhere in the atmosphere, was her carefree girlhood. Behind the locked door stood a woman filled with the grief of separation, the yearning for her beloved.

'And all the while you grieved,' Nut smiled. 'Osiris was determined to win you completely. As he sailed to see us, he was still wondering if you wanted him. But he was bent on his journey.'

- 'I will travel north in the boat, carrying my bundle of reeds, to Memphis. There I'll confess to Ptah, lord of truth, that Eset is my only love. I will entreat him: Give me my sister tonight, my lord. The river is like wine, its rushes are mighty Ptah, its foliage the great lioness Sekhmet, goddesses in buds, and lotus blossoms. The golden Hathor joyfully brightens the earth with her blessings. All Memphis is a bowl of fruit placed before my love, the fair-of-face. And if, after gaining the approval of the Ennead – the nine Great Ones – Eset still refuses me, then I shall lie down and become ill. My sister will come then, for she is powerful in medicine. The physicians will not be needed, only she understands my illness.'

'Ptah told Osiris that you were not like the sisters and brothers born to humankind where love between siblings is forbidden, that the lords of creation have different rules: in order to pass on their greatness, they must procreate. He reminded Osiris that you were the children of the primordial couple – Geb, my brother, and I. And I reminded him how we loved and clung to each other until Tefnut, the Atmosphere, separated us. Then we bore you with Osiris, Set with Nephthys. As couples, bound together by cosmic duty, you were destined to make love. It is your love that will create human leaders and they will be called pharaohs. You and Osiris will be incarnate in them and they, too, will marry brother to sister.'

'I was sick from love, Mother,' Eset murmured. 'I forgot about everything but the power and surge of passion and union. How unyielding I was when Osiris returned. I would not let him in. My passion threw me into such confusion I felt fear and anger and desire and shame all at once. But he stood at my door, calling out, unconcerned that someone might hear.'

- 'I stand at my sister's mansion. The door-leaves are open but the bolt is sprung. Eset is angry with me. If I were her doorkeeper, I would enter and make her rage at me.'

- Eset heard his voice, and came to the window. 'How can you dare to sing at my door?' she called down.
- 'Is my singing offensive? It was the sweetest sound to you once. Why are you angry with me?'
- 'You left me. You floated out of sight, away from me, without saying goodbye. You abandoned me without a word of explanation.'
- 'Abandoned you? I have never abandoned you!'
- Eset disappeared from the window, flew down to the door, unbolted it, hurling herself at the amazed Osiris.
- 'You left before our quarrel was resolved.' She clawed at him, like a wild woman. Osiris squeezed his arms through hers, cupping her cheeks and stroking them, firmly, smoothly. He dried her tears, took the strands of waving hair from her eyes and pinned them back behind her ears.
- 'Sssh,' he whispered. 'Listen to me, my love. Listen to me. I went to resolve the quarrel once and for all. I could never abandon you. Weren't we created together? I could no longer be separated from you by the rules of others. That was why I went.'
- Eset looked up at him, lips parted. 'Where did you go?' she sobbed. 'And why were you so long in coming back?'
- 'I went north to see Ptah. I wanted to claim you openly and proudly before the Ennead. I wanted it settled that you are mine as I am yours. Together and apart.'
- 'Together,' Eset murmured, 'always together. I cannot be separated from you, Osiris. I don't have your strength.'

But now she is trapped in a sort of nowhereland of separation, wandering in search of him. Looking for signs – some song, some fragrance, some icon – in her solitary non-existence, an itinerant face like her own, mourning its lost half. As the years pass, Eset feels an innate conviction that children will give her the clues to Osiris' whereabouts, children, the holders of the Four Parts, within the body, the life force *Ka*, the spirit *Ba*, the two together united, making *akh*, the unification, and then *shuwt* or *khou*, the inevitable shadow. Yes, they stay close to the createdness, still allied to their instincts, their inner eye. They watch the shadows, see through blackness. She tells the children stories that fill their minds with her yearning. They speak to her but they cannot tell her enough.

She wanders on, searching, searching, until one day she arrives in a small, desert village. In the distance, at the foot of the temple steps, she spies a child. He sits alone, apart from the others, his writing block on the step before him.

'If I tell you a story, will you look into the future for me?'

- The great sun-king was preparing to go to his brother's feast. Eset, his sister, did not approve.
- 'Why should you go?' she demanded. 'Our brother Set is nothing but trouble. What could you wish to celebrate with him?'
- Osiris was perplexed. 'He's extending the hand of friendship, Eset. Why hurt him? He is our brother. I don't want to be his enemy.'
- Eset veiled her anger. 'You are the All-King, Osiris, you should be a better judge. Will you never learn to protect yourself?'
- Osiris dropped a brief kiss on her hair. It was so gentle. He looked perplexed, a little hurt. Then he was gone.

- Oh, Osiris, she thought tenderly, I spoke out of love. I can't be everywhere to protect you. Be safe and come back whole and soon.

- Osiris entered the hall of Set's mansion. It was filled with faces he did not know. But everyone knew Osiris; the Great Teacher, Spreader of Wisdom, Grower of Grain.

- When the celebrations were at their height, people feasting on magnificent foods, drinking the rich ruby wines, ten men entered carrying on their shoulders a magnificent trunk. 'What could that be?' the question buzzed around the room. 'What surprise has Set planned for his guests?'

- They did not have to wait long. Set took his position beside the chest and clapped his hands grandly.

- 'Companions,' he shouted. His sharp, metallic voice almost shook with excitement as no king's ever would. 'Do you see this splendid chest? I ordered it specially. I ordered it for your pleasure. Now, any of you here present has the right to win this chest. There is only one condition. You must lie down in it first. He whose body fits it may take it home.'

- Straightaway Set's guests began to climb in and out. 'Set wants to appear generous – but without giving away the jewelled chest,' the disgruntled guests muttered.

- As midnight approached most had tried it and found it too big. Finally, only Osiris was left.

- Set came to him. 'Brother, have you tried your luck?'

- Osiris laughed. 'My luck? No, Set. I don't need a chest, though I admit it is beautifully made.'

- 'It's a game, big brother,' Set teased. 'Still too sober to play games? I remember as a child how you tried to find the greater purpose behind a simple game. Ah, well, I

hoped age would mellow you, give you a lighter heart –
and that with the delicious Eset at your side your taste for
fun would develop. But think nothing of it.' He turned to
walk away.

- Osiris squeezed his brother's shoulder. 'What a bad guest
  I am, Set. Of course I'll play your game.'

- Set looked triumphant. He snatched Osiris' hand and led
  him almost at a run to the dais on which the chest stood.
  With a flourish he commanded his men to open the hinged
  lid. Six large men bent to heave it up and laid it back
  carefully.

- Osiris stepped forward and looked into its hollow darkness. He felt a flash of discomfort. The box was like a
  sarcophagus but hardly bigger than his bed. Well, he
  would climb in. That was not too much to do for his
  brother. Set had been charming and attentive all evening.
  He raised himself over the side of the chest and laid himself down in its base.

- A gasp went up in the hall – a perfect fit – followed by the
  thought that Set had made the chest to accommodate his
  brother because he wanted to get back into his favour. But
  while the usual suspicious thoughts were circulating
  through the room, Set's six giants had clapped the lid in
  place and were binding the box with iron chains and locks
  with Osiris still inside.

- And as the startled guests watched, ten men carried out
  the chest and marched with it to the Nile, careful to take
  a route that did not pass the palace. Set had told his men
  that he did not care if all the people of Egypt witnessed
  the act – they were powerless. But Eset, eternal guardian
  of Osiris, All-Queen, powerful woman of magic, must at

all costs be kept ignorant of events. Once Osiris was carried to the Nile in the sarcophagus, cut adrift to float on the seat, to die a slow asphyxiating death, leaving Set to take over Egypt, no doubt she would find out.

- And Eset, woman of magic, tossed and turned in her bed all night, tormented, thinking: He has not come back. I wounded him and now he is staying away from me. Tomorrow I'll go to him in Set's house. I'll give him healing medicines and show him my love. He'll see my open door and return to our palace.

- But Osiris never came back. Eset heard the story the next day. She dressed in mourning, slashed off her hair and set out in search of her husband. She roamed from city to city, through the desert and along the shorelines, in the mountains and in the valleys and in every wilderness. She has wandered endlessly searching for Osiris for so many years that small children have grown up, hearing from birth of the Weeping Woman. The Weeping Woman, the Seeking Lover whose quest never ends.

She can see her own thoughts reflected in the boy's mind and knows that he can help her if he truly listens. She knows this from the wisdom in his young eyes, once old, in which his ancient spirit still survives.

'I saw the sarcophagus, the same one you described. It washed up on the shores of a river.'

Eset's hand flashes out, grasps his wrist but he doesn't flinch. 'The Nile?' she asks. 'Which part of the Nile?'

'I don't know,' the boy replies. 'Just a shore somewhere, by a temple where the king's people come and go. It is washed up into the rushes. I see it resting up against a sapling.'

'That might be any riverbank,' Eset replies softly. She moves closer to the boy, enfolds his body in hers, draws him towards her until his back, the curve of his body fits hers. She the throne, he the occupant. For now he is her Osiris. She puts her hand on his forehead, caressing him. She draws his head back upon her shoulder and lays her other hand over his eyes. He feels as if waves are lapping him. 'Close your eyes and see with your mind. Listen with the Eye of Hathor, absorb with the Eye of Amun the Sun.'

The boy does as she says. 'First it left the Nile and launched upon the Great Sea.'

The vitality goes out of Eset. 'The sea? He could be anywhere in the world.'

The boy garners in all the power from the edges of his body to the centre of his being. 'The river is on the shores of a place called . . . Byblos.'

Eset holds him, cradles him, kisses the still closed, sweet, wise eyes that have seen her love. 'Your life will be filled with sweetness and knowledge,' she says. 'You will be loved by all who set eyes on you. You will be a chosen one of Eset.'

'Eset?' The boy's eyes fly open. 'You?'

Eset rises. 'Now I must go.'

The Weeping Woman sits on the edge of a fountain by a well, sad, wild. Her eyes scour the reeded sands of the river flowing past this stretch of Byblos. She has searched, how she has searched, for the sarcophagus, the sapling against which the boy-scribe said it rested – but she has found nothing. Yet the rest fits his description exactly. The temple, the fountain, it is merely a matter of time now before someone arrives. Eset gets up, walks up and down. She sees a large, devastated mound, a vast crater, crawling with roots and insects and covered with dead reeds and rushes. Eset reaches down into the crater, withdraws her hand, crumbling the soil between her fingertips. Slowly she brings her fingers to her nose and inhales the deep, rich fragrance of the earth. It is the smell of ambrosia. This must be where the tree once grew that sheltered Osiris. Who had removed the sarcophagus? The boy-scribe had spoken of the 'king's people'. Perhaps they had seen the jewelled chest and the tree that protected it. The ambrosia-scented sand tells her the tree was suffused with divine fragrance as a reward for providing Osiris with a haven. No doubt they had decided to remove it to the palace. Who would leave such things out in the wilderness?

Eset returns to the fountain. Clearly, she must visit the palace of the King of Byblos and inquire after the jewelled sarcophagus that held her lover. She will strike a bargain. They can keep the sarcophagus and all the riches inside and she will take Osiris. Her heart soars at the thought of touching that beloved form again, and for moments she is lost in reverie.

And here come some women! Skittish, laughing, playful, they make their way to the steps of the temple. They are lavishly dressed, their jars and pots are clearly of high quality. 'The king's people,' the boy had said.

Slowly, Eset rises to her feet. She glides towards the water's edge, laves her face with water, smoothes her clothes, runs a magic hand over herself. Then she takes up her position by the temple porch. They remain in the temple for an hour or two. But what's that to Eset, who has roamed for years, searching for her lost love? She is unaware of time as she stands in its still eternity, waiting. The women come out and see Eset. They stop, enchanted by this mysterious woman, dark, beautiful and still, so very still.

Eset smiles, raises a hand in salutation. The women turn as one and form a semicircle around her.

'Who are you, beautiful one?' asks a tall, plump girl.

'I am Eset of Philae,' she replies. 'Who are you?'

'We are the queen's handmaidens. We have come to carry back some jars of blessed water to bathe and purify her. She has just given birth to a second son.'

Eset inclines her head. 'She is fortunate to be blessed with two children.'

'And what is your work here, Eset of Philae?'

Eset laughs a soft, deep, soundless laugh that runs through the women and through the earth. 'My work? Ah, mine is a long and ancient quest. I am the Searching Woman. But come, young women of the city, and let me groom you. Let me style your hair and make you fragrant with my breath.'

She holds out her arms and one by one the women come to her and allow her to groom and plait their hair, to smooth their skin and breathe ambrosia over them so that a mystical fragrance wafts from them whenever they move. Enchanted, they make their way to the palace of King Malcathros, carrying jars of water to bathe their queen.

When they have gone, Eset waits and watches until a cloud of dust in the distance assembles in her vision. It grows thicker, then slowly settles. A figure alights. The women Eset groomed earlier cluster around her. They glow and shimmer, dimming the queen's light as they lead their mistress towards Eset.

'You are Eset,' the queen says. 'I came here to see you.'

Eset does not bow, noting the surprise on the queen's face.

'I am Astarte, Queen of Byblos. I want you to groom me as you groomed my serving women.'

Eset smiles. 'Come,' she says. 'Sit here, at my knee.'

The queen kneels on the ground without demur. She is in a trance. Eset tends her. She combs through her hair, oils and braids it, cleans and anoints her skin. She draws lines of antimony around her eyes, covers her lids in the purest of crushed lapis lazuli enhanced with gold dust, reddens her lips with unguents extracted from red stone and the dyes of vegetables and fruit. Then when she is finished, she enfolds Astarte in both arms and breathes deeply. The queen's skin begins to gleam, and the atmosphere is heady with ambrosial scent.

Queen Astarte looks up at Eset, sloe-eyed. 'Come with me to my palace, Searching Woman,' she entreats. 'I have work for you. You must look after my new infant. My young son.'

Eset inclines her head in agreement. She is accepting the job of a servant, but her gesture is imperious, gracious.

'Sit beside me in the carriage,' Astarte says.

Her women stare, astonished as she hands Eset up to the attendant and follows. 'The queen is bewitched,' they whisper among themselves.

The baby leaps from his mother's arms into Eset's, like a wave leaping back into the sea, and melds into her, water into water. The king and queen are surprised but happy.

'The infant prince will be happy,' the kings says. 'You have chosen well, Astarte.'

Eset takes the child into her arms and feels a surge of emotion. She was meant to be a mother. Now perhaps she will never be. She turns to follow a woman standing ready to lead her to the infant prince's chamber. The child flails his little arms and Eset's eye is drawn to one of the tall columns reaching up to the palace roof. It is different from the rest. Its wood comes from the tamarisk tree while the others are cedar. She glides towards it in a daze as the infant gurgles and crows, leaning his body away from her arms and towards the column. Eset follows where he leads The infant strokes the column gleefully, attempting to embrace it, but his arms can span only a small part of its front surface as he rests his mouth against its polished exterior. The saliva from his mouth mixes with it and produces a strong scent.

'Osiris,' Eset breathes. 'You've led me to Osiris.'

Eset does not know how Osiris and the tamarisk tree are united but she knows now that it contains his essence. She will reward the boy for leading her to it. She will give him immortality. Every night as Eset ponders the question of Osiris' presence in the column, she transforms herself into a sparrow-hawk and circles around the infant, creating a magic blaze of fire to burn away his mortality. The infant will be immortal: he can stay in this world, enjoying its transient pleasures, but he will have a bridge into the Other World. Perhaps he will also be her guide to Osiris.

In the deep of the night when the boy sleeps, Eset works her magic. Patiently, she circles around him burning away the finely meshed cage of intangible threads that tug and pull the mortal parts towards illness, disease and decay. Slowly, the cocoon that binds his small form to the world of phenomena dissolves. At last, there remains only the lower husk clinging to his back like a gossamer eggshell. Eset plunges herself into the final ritual. She feels the blood hum and sing within her body as she changes herself into the bird and begins to fly. As she encircles him, her glossy wings fan the magic blaze behind her forked tail feathers. Before dawn arrives, he will be immortal. Free of bonds, free of human bondage, shining eternally.

A shriek shatters her ritual.

Astarte rushes through the fire-ring and snatches up her infant. Eset stands beside the cot, weeping. It is never to be. She watches the silver-grey threads reappear, knitting themselves instantaneously around the child, tethering him to his mortality. It is never to be.

'You evil creature!' Astarte screams. 'I trusted you with my child. I was good to you. I honoured you. And you're trying to kill him.'

Eset's jet eyes hold the ritual fire, blazing, flaring, as she directs her gaze at Astarte. The foolish woman laments and wails. 'My child, my poor helpless child. You were burning my child, you sorceress.'

'Foolish, foolish woman,' Eset says at last. 'I am Eset, Queen of Egypt, mother of humanity. Your child would have been immortal. You have destroyed my ritual.'

But Astarte does not understand. Her screams bring Malcathros to the chamber. His eyes are fixed on Eset, tall, luminous, a tower of ivory, lapis, silver and gold. The mirage that concealed her identity has lifted. He falls to his knees.

'Eset,' he cries, his head at her feet. 'All-Powerful One. The *One*, the sister without peer. Forgive Astarte. Forgive us both.'

Eset's heart fills with mercy. She can never punish the penitent.

'Tell me how I can atone for our sins. Take anything you want from me. Just leave me my family. Is there anything I can offer that is worthy of you?'

'The column of tamarisk in your court.' Eset's voice is soft.

'The perfumed column?'

Eset inclines her head.

'It is yours.'

'I will leave with it tomorrow.'

'Tomorrow? But, Great Queen, the column supports the entire structure of my palace. I will need time.'

Eset smiles and the room fills with warmth. 'Your palace will stand firm by my will.'

Once again King Malcathros lays his head at her feet. 'Your will be done.'

In the hall, Eset effortlessly removes the pillar from its location, cuts away the trunk of the tamarisk tree releasing its fragrance into the air. Inside she finds the sealed sarcophagus. She removes it and returns the tree trunk to its original position.

'Know,' Eset says, as she walks past Astarte and Malcathros, touching their core with her presence, 'your child might have been the first human to become immortal. But so be it. He will still lead a good life.'

Then she is gone.

The Nile is dark and smooth-flowing. On her boat, Eset, luminous like the moon, swathed in the waters of her grief, stands by the open sarcophagus. Its gems catch her light as she stirs and glint back at her like celestial spheres. Inside, in the dark depths, lies Osiris. His silence is her failure, his stillness her wound. She cries out in pain, lowering herself into the sarcophagus. She strokes his cheeks, but his inert body does not respond.

'Oh, my love,' she cries, laying her body over his motionless form, so peaceful and soft. He is not dead, just asleep, he could not have left life. She feels it within him. Her face hovers above his. Then she rests her cheek against his, feeling this still energy. She raises her face, covers his in caresses, slowly, surely, brushing his forehead with her lips, scattering soft kisses on his eyes, down his cheeks, then clasping his face firmly between her palms, a firm, slow greeting on his mouth.

Her soul speaks to his. He will answer. He has always answered her.

'Do you remember when I was angry with you? You would lie down and be sick. The physicians would crowd your bed and the word would be out that Osiris is ill, the Brother is ill. And as soon as I heard the words, I would put aside everything – my food lay uneaten, my hair was unbraided, my feet were unclad – and I would run to you, my beloved spouse. The first time, the physicians would not move to make way for me. I was helpless. Nut, our mother, glowered at me, like lightning ready to strike. Geb, our father, frowned at me as if a hundred stormclouds would break on me. I hardly noticed. My heart was beating to be near you. But they stood in my way. And then you spoke. Do you remember what you said?'

'I am sick from love. My sister was angry. But now she is here. I need no physician. She understands my illness. She knows the cure.'

'And I replied: "I am the cure." They parted then and let

me through. I placed my cheek on yours, kissed your head, your eyes, your lips.'

'And I arose.' Osiris' voice echoes in the atmosphere.

'Will you rise now?' Eset knows his reply deeply within herself.

'I cannot, my beloved.'

Eset buries her face in his neck. 'Cannot, Osiris?'

'What I would give to be by your side as you want me, Eset.'

'Does your new world draw you so strongly that you cannot return to me?'

'It holds me,' he replied, his voice fading. 'It is where my body is retained and re-formed. But if only you knew it, my love, my Eset, I am more with you now, in spirit, in presence, than I have ever been before.'

She can sense the pain of his conflict – the struggle she is creating within him. She is questioning his acceptance of his function in the cosmic order. She knows she will never possess him again as she did before.

'Believe that I am yours everywhere, at all times. If only you could know it.'

'Let me heal your wounds,' she says. 'My medicines always healed you. My magic never failed before.'

She rises, unclothes his wounded body, rubs sweet-scented oils resolutely, smoothly, on his limbs. Her fingers mould his feet, his legs, and thighs. They hover over his stomach, tip to tip, palpating, rubbing, stimulating, then pass over his chest, slowly encircling his golden nipples. Instinctively, she bends her head to his scars, kissing them, sealing them with her tongue, watching them disappear. She is lying beside him now, as she has so many times before, recalling how he sometimes grew inert with the pleasure of her ministrations, limbs heavy with the gratification of desire. Then, too, she felt he was there and not there, in her bed, touching her body, but somehow formless. With a moan, half ecstasy, half wrenching torment, she smothers his throat in kisses. Osiris will respond. Very soon, Osiris will rise, turn her over, and return her ministrations, demanding, almost fierce at first, then tender and rhythmic as the song of the waves lapping against her. Her desire always inflames Osiris. She buries her fingers in the hair at the nape of his neck, her arms encircling him as she writhes against his body and waits, expectant.

Osiris does not move. Eset raises herself to look at his face, her forearms resting lightly on his healed chest. Did she see his eyelids flutter? The twitch of a smile on his mouth? Is this a new game Osiris is playing to extend her pleasure? She peers into his face, then recoils with a gasp. She has seen a veil flutter between them. An Otherworld veil that separates her irrevocably from him.

'Why must you torment him?' a voice asks. 'Why do you try to shame him back into worldly life?'

'Neith?' Eset's voice is a whisper.

'It is I. Neith of the temple Sais.'

'I saw your veil separating him from me.'

'Ah, Eset. You have not grasped my mystery. If only you could see which side of the veil you are on, you would not lament and strive so.'

'Why must he be taken from me?'

'Taken from you? Osiris travelled the world without you, teaching, preaching, civilizing and changing the world. Did you think then that he had abandoned you? No, he was doing his duty, fulfilling his predestined task. This is no different. Yet you weep and wail and roam the world aimlessly, wreaking devastation, demanding his return.'

'But then I knew he was alive and would come back.'

'Do you think he is dead now?'

Eset gazes at Osiris' body. 'He is not?'

'He is more alive, more free, more vibrant than ever before.'

'I don't understand.'

'Your work on earth is not finished. Stop clamouring for Osiris, look to your duties. You are the throne, the protectress of Egypt's sovereignty. Do your work.'

Neith's veils whirl around her, diaphanous shadows catching the moon's glow and shining for an instant, before vanishing. And on the rustle of the garments, Eset hears the cryptic, whispered message of Neith: 'When you solve the mystery, you will no longer yearn. Death and distance are states of mind. You have still to find the continuum.

'I am all that has been, that is, that will be, and no mortal has been able to lift the veil that covers me. But you, Eset, will one day become part of my mysteries. When your work is done. When you remember you are not mortal.'

Eset throws herself on Osiris once more. This time she cradles him gently in her arms, remembering their tenderest moments, their sweetest words. In the distance a sulky dawn begins reluctantly to manifest.

Eset lays down her lover's head and stands gazing at him, chanting the words of a spell under her breath. In moments she has metamorphosed into a falcon. Her feathers shine, her eyes glitter like gems and the whirring of her wings is like a heavenly song. Around and around and around and around, she circles Osiris, breathing from every particle of her bird form. Her breath is like the morning breeze, gently reviving and enlivening the deepest sleeper with its magical kiss. Osiris stirs. She comes closer, still revolving. She can see Osiris has awoken. She will have her moment with him. With a soft cry, she places her body against his. At last, at last, there is life in him again. His body throbs and pulsates, grows. But he does not turn her over this time, gently easing her on to him so that they are meshed together as they lie. Moving, moving together, exquisite in their plumage. In Eset's eyes appears a large blue bud, tightly furled. She sees his face through sealed lids as tremors of bliss vibrate through her body. She sees the bud burst open: it showers its seeds outwards. There is a swell in her belly. She flies back, reeling with the energy bolts she has experienced. When she looks down again, Osiris is motionless.

She returns to her natural form – Eset, the Great One. She has still to understand what has happened between them, what has passed. All she knows is that she has succeeded in performing part of the cosmic function of which Neith spoke: her task in the human world.

Eset returns to her native land but remains in the forest edging the Nile. She makes a dwelling of reeds and grass, a mattress of foliage, a pillow of feathers. She conceals Osiris in his sarcophagus deep in a mound of compacted sand covered in grass and scrub, strewn with sea-flowers. She stays away from Set. She searches for food during the day, and at night she lies awake, pondering her next move, recalling Neith's injunction. Tonight Osiris fills her mind even more than usual.

Eset writhes in her bed. She flings her head to one side of her pillow, then the other. Her flushed, hot cheeks seek a cool place. She sees the Nile, hostile, punishing, rise higher and higher. It roars. Above its angry roar, she hears a deep, musical voice.

> My sister's love is on yonder side
> The river is between our bodies;
> The waters are mighty at flood time,
> A crocodile waits in the shallows.
> My sister has come, my heart exults,
> My arms spread out to embrace her;
> My heart bounds in its place,
> Like the red fish in the pond.
> Oh, night, be mine for ever,
> Now that the queen has come.

'Osiris!' Eset cries. 'Here, Osiris. I'm here.'

Across the waters, now calmer, she sees her lover, her brother and holds out her arms. 'Come to me, Osiris. I'm here.'

Osiris is all in shadow as she strains to see him. 'Why won't you come, Osiris? You know I can't come to you.'

> I enter the water and brave the waves,
> My heart is strong in the deep;
> The crocodile does not frighten me,
> The flood is as land to my feet.
> It is her love that gives me strength,
> It makes a water-spell for me;
> I gaze at my heart's desire.
> As she stands facing me!

Suddenly, the river disappears and Eset sees her beloved at the top of a hillock. The shadow of a pear tree shades him and she watches the petals of its blossom like raindrops, gently falling, creating a veil around him. She feels the familiar pull in her heart. How she longs to see his face in the light. How she longs to dispel the distance deepened by the darkness which seemed to surround him now.

'Let me see you, Sun of Egypt,' her heart cries out, 'let me see you again.'

She closes her eyes as the hot tears collect, then begin coursing slowly down her cheeks. She strokes the chill clinging to her arms. Suddenly, it is dispelled. Warmth spills over her like the heat from a brazier. What new trick is fate playing on her now? Eset opens her eyes, wary of some new misfortune.

Her hand flies to her eyes. The sun is shining bright and hot. The pine trees feel it too: its warmth wafts their perfume gently to her nostrils. And there, in full glory, stands Osiris. Oh, how she weeps to see his sweet face. She takes a few faltering steps towards him, then holds back. What if he disintegrates, like a dream, like smoke? What will she do then? She will linger here, send him her tenderness, savour his substantial form. She will not come too close in case the nearness takes him from her again. Osiris is standing not ten feet from her. He holds out his arms and she longs to go into them. But still she hesitates.

'Are you angry with me, my sister?'

'Angry?' Eset's voice holds a sob and a laugh. 'Angry with you? How could I be?'

Osiris smiles as if he has guessed something. 'You are with child?'

Eset touches her body tenderly. 'Why do you say that?'

'You are like a tree in the full splendour of early spring – youth, full of sap. Your hair is glossy as new, tender foliage. Your eyes are like the flowers that precede the fruit. You are to bear fruit.' He holds out his hands and allows a pile of petals to collect in them, creamy white, like feathers.

'Your child. Do you approve?'

'Oh, Eset, Eset, how can it be otherwise?'

Eset's eyes are full of grief. She is running towards him now, no longer caring whether he is a spectre or a creature of substance, stopping only when she is so near she can feel the puffs of air caused by his movements. Then there is stillness.

'Can I touch you?' Her eyes are troubled.

'Touch me.' Osiris' breath is hot on Eset's cheek. 'Touch me, my love. I'm here beside you.'

Eset falls against Osiris' breast. 'I can't lose you again.'

Osiris embraces her now, his strong, familiar arms holding her firmly against him. For a long time he rests his cheek against the crown of her head. He kisses her hair, her forehead, her eyes. 'You are troubled,' he says. 'Why? I came to bring you peace.'

'I know we must part again.'

'Ah, my love,' he sighs, with the withheld sorrow of a hundred separations, 'we die just once. That death is over. If only you knew that I am always with you. It is not the body that matters, it is the essence. And now you hold that in your body.'

A lament strangles in Eset's throat. 'I know, I know,' she cries. 'What you say must be true. But now, here, your words feel empty. I want you like this, Osiris, always like this.'

She holds him firmly, close, knowing he is going to leave.

'Alone,' she breathes, her eyes opening against her pillow, 'you'll walk alone again. Without me.'

'But your presence is with me, beloved.' The whisper comes to her across sleep, across the water, across the infinite void. 'Surely you feel me, even if you can't see me? I can feel you. My love, my essence is with you always. As yours remains with me.'

In the distance, a shadow drifts away, surrounded by many suns.

But her pillow is cool against her flushed cheek now. Osiris has been with her. In her bed. He has left with her a new strength. Her worldly mission grows in her womb, the child Osiris, Horus the first king, whom she will enthrone. Then she will be free to travel all worlds.

The pain of separation is mist water, nothing before the sun.

The Ballad of Skirnir

*It is intriguing how people in fairytales fall in love with
an image or an idea. The turmoil and the huge risks
taken to achieve union reflect the intensity of desire for the
love-object. The erotic element lies in the quest.*

Freyr, the son of Njorth, sat one day in Hlithiskjolf, the
throne of Odin, and surveyed all the worlds. He looked into
Jotunheim, Land of the Giants, where he saw a beautiful
maiden on her way from her father's palace to her flower
grove. He was instantly consumed by a potent love-sickness.
Freyr's servant was called Skirnir. Njorth summoned him
and commanded him to speak to Freyr.

> *Njorth:*
> Go at once, Skirnir! And try to get
> An answer from my son.
> Ask him: who enrages him,
> Who has made him sulk?

> *Skirnir:*
> Your son will reply angrily
> If I try to get an answer

by asking: who enrages him
Who has made him sulk?

Speak, please, Freyr, greatest among the gods
I want to know why you
Sit alone, in these wide halls,
My prince, for days?

Freyr:
Why should I tell you, young hero,
Of my grief, so dark
That even the elfbeam rising
Each morning, does not dispel my gloom?

Skirnir:
Your grief may not be too terrible
To confide to me;
Since once we were young lads together
We could perhaps still trust each other.

Freyr:
Coming out of Gymir's palace, I saw
A young woman – I fell in love.
Her arms glittered and their gleam
Made all the sea and sky shine.

I love her more than any man
Ever loved a woman.
But there is not a god or an elf
Who approves of our coming together.

Skirnir:

Then give me a horse
That will brave the magic, flickering flames,
And a sword that will fight on its own
Against the merciless giants.

Freyr:

I give you the horse
That will brave the magic, flickering flames
And a sword that will fight on its own,
When wielded by a worthy hero.

Skirnir:

It is dark outside and, I think, time
To set off through the untamed downs
To traverse the Land of Giants.
If I do not return with her
The terrible giant will have destroyed us both.

Through the Land of the Giants, Skirnir rode to Gymir's palace. Ferocious dogs stood chained by the gate of the fence which bounded Gerth's house. Skirnir rode to a herdsman sitting on a hill.

Skirnir:

Tell me, herdsman, sitting on the hill,
And watching the roads below,
How can I get past Gymir's dogs
And talk to his daughter inside?

Herdsman:
Is death stalking you or are you already dead?
There is not a chance
That you'll ever speak
To Gymir's virtuous daughter.

Skirnir:
Courage is better than complaints
To a determined man.
My death, after all, is confined to a single moment.
Until then my life-span will go on.

Gerth:
What is that loud noise
I can hear inside our house?
There's a tremor in the ground and Gymir's palace
Is shuddering around me.

Serving maid:
A man stands outside
He has just leapt from his horse
And set it loose to graze.

Gerth:
Tell him to come in
And drink some of our fine mead,
Though I am afraid that the man outside
Will turn out to be my brother's murderer.

Are you an elf or a son of the gods
Or one of the wise Vanirs?

How did you manage single-handedly
to defy the blazing inferno and enter our home?

Skirnir:
I am not an elf, nor the son of the gods.
Nor am I a wise Vanir.
Still I managed single-handedly
To come through the blazing inferno.

I have eleven healing-apples made of gold.
I will give them to you, Gerth,
In return for a pledge from you
To love Freyr above all creatures.

Gerth:
I would never accept those eleven apples
To please any man.
Nor could Freyr and I come together
As long as we live.

Skirnir:
Then I offer you the ring that was burned
With Odin's son Baldur at his funeral.
Eight more of the same weight
Drop from it every ninth night.

Gerth:
I do not want the ring,
Though it was burned with Odin's son Baldur.
There is no shortage of gold in Gymir's home
In the riches he controls.

Skirnir:

Do you see this sharp, bright sword, young woman
That I hold here in my hand?
I will use it to chop your head from your neck
If you refuse to do my will.

Gerth:

From no man will I ever tolerate
Such an intimidating show of force.
But I am sure that Gymir would be happy to fight
   you
If he found you here.

Skirnir:

Do you see this sharp, bright sword, young woman
That I hold here in my hand?
Before its blade, the old giant will bow down.
Your father's death will be inevitable.

I strike you, young woman, with my magic staff,
To bend you to my demand.
You will be banished to a place
Where no man can see you.

You'll sit for ever on Eagle's Hill,
Gazing at Hell's gates,
Your flesh as loathsome to men
As a poisonous snake.

Terrifying to see when you come out,
Drawing the contemptuous stares

Of Frost-giant Hrimnir and all others,
You'll be more notorious than Heimdal,
   watchman of the gods.

Raging against chains of fury
Yearning for release, tortured tears flowing
Wherever you sit, my curse will follow
And double your misery.

In the giant's house, vile things will wound you
Day after relentless day.
You will grieve without relief.
Instead of happiness, you'll face suffering.

With three-headed giants as eternal companions
You'll never find a husband.
May you be gripped with desire, wasted with
   longing,
May you be like the thistle thrown in a loft and
   crushed.

Now I will go to the woods, young woman,
To the moist forests,
To find a magic staff.
I have found a magic staff.

Odin, mightiest god, is angry with you.
Freyr will become your enemy,
You evil woman,
Bent on drawing the wrath of gods to yourself.

Listen to me, frost-giants, listen, giants,
Sons of Suttung, and all you gods too,
How I forbid and how I ban from this
    woman
The joyful sounds of men's passion.

Instead, the frost-shrouded giant
    Hrimgrimnar will possess you
In the gloomy depths of Hell's gates.
Each day you'll go to the Frost-giant's doors,
Crawling with desperate desire.

Vile beings there by the root of the tree
Will feed you filthy food,
And you'll find nothing better anywhere,
Young woman, if you persist in your wish.

I will write you a charm with three runes:
Longing and Madness and Lust.
But I can erase them
If I ever need to.

Gerth:
Then I welcome you and offer
A chilled cup of mead,
Though I never believed that I would so love
One of the Vanir.

Skirnir:
Then tell me openly,
Before I return home,

How soon will you come to the mighty son
Of Njorth to unite with him?

Gerth:
The forest of Barri, which we both know well,
Is a beautiful and serene forest.
Nine nights from now, I will meet the son of Njorth,
And there I'll grant him delight.

Then Skirnir rode home. Freyr stood outside, waiting for him. He asked Skirnir for news.

Freyr:
Tell me, Skirnir, before you dismount
Or take another step.
What have you achieved in the Land of Giants
To gladden my heart or yours?

Skirnir:
In the forest of Barri, which we both know well,
A beautiful and serene forest,
Nine nights from now, she will meet the son of Njorth
And there she'll grant him delight.

Freyr:
One night is interminable, two even more,
How can I survive three?
I've lived through months that felt shorter
Than half a night of this burning desire.

Maui

Love triangles are a high-risk game of chance. But if it's got to happen, I can't think of a better lover with whom to play it than Maui, the terrific trickster from the South Pacific.

Now, in the land under the sea lived the Monster Eel, known as Te Tuna which means 'The Penis'. In the frigid torpor of his land, he was slow in motion, slow to respond, a fact that was not lost on his beautiful consort, Hina. So, on the pretext of setting out to look for food for the two of them, Hina went off one day seeking lovers to match her passion.

She soon arrived at the distant land of the Male-Principle Clan and called out her intentions, announcing that she had left the disappointing and insipid Te Tuna, and sought an eel-shaped rod of love.

'I am the dark and shameless pubic patch seeking the release of desire,' she said. 'I have come a long way for this, so let your staffs rise up tumescent and plunge into love's consummation.'

'Oh, no,' shouted the men of the clan. 'Te Tuna would kill us if we did. There is the road – keep going.'

So Hina journeyed on, her loins aflame, and was rebuffed twice more until she came to the land of the Maui Clan, the wonder-workers, and repeated her challenging call. Now, Maui himself had fished up the very islands from the sea, had slowed down the sun in its passage, and lifted the sky off the earth to make room for people to live. He had stolen fire for his mother to use in her kitchen, and she was always on the lookout for ways to reward his heroic acts. So when she saw Hina approaching, she told Maui to bestir himself and take the beautiful stranger for his own.

Needing no further prompting, Maui claimed Hina and they lived together in exquisite passion there for many days. But then people realized this was Te Tuna's wife sporting in their midst and went to tell the Monster Eel. Te Tuna merely shrugged torpidly saying that Maui could have her. But people continued to gossip to him about Hina until, finally, he got angry.

'What is this Maui like,' he asked contemptuously, 'this mere man?'

'He's not very big,' the gossips said, 'and the end of his penis is lopsided.'

'Well, let him get a look at this,' Te Tuna said, waving the soiled loincloth that hung between his legs, 'and he will fly away.'

The people reported to Maui that Te Tuna was coming for revenge and Maui, unconcerned, asked what sort of creature Te Tuna was. An enormous monster, they replied.

'Is he sturdy, strong as an upright tree?' Maui asked, and the gossips explained that he was like a leaning tree, ever bent. But they remained fearful, since this was the first time anyone could remember when someone had stolen the wife of another. 'We will all be killed,' they moaned, but Maui told them not to worry.

Sure enough, the skies soon darkened, lightning tore at the heavens and thunder boomed across the surface of the earth. Te Tuna, the Penis, approached in fury, accompanied by four other monsters. He stripped off his disgusting loin-cloth and held it high, and as he did so, the sea surged high and a towering wall of water surged toward the land. The people recoiled in panic, but Maui's mother shouted to her son: 'Quick! Show him yours!'

So Maui loosed his lopsided penis and raised it against the surging waters. The wave subsided, leaving the monsters high and dry on a reef, and Maui leapt on them and dispatched them – all but Te Tuna, whom he spared. Instead, he invited the Monster Eel to share his house.

There was a period of harmony but, of course, it could not last. One day, Te Tuna said a duel was necessary, the winner to take Hina exclusively for himself. First, he said, there must be a contest in which each entered the body of the other. After that, he said, 'I'll kill you and take Hina home to my land beneath the sea.' Again, Maui shrugged, and told Te Tuna to go first.

So chanting a song, and swinging and swaying his head, the Monster Eel grew smaller and smaller and disappeared into Maui's body, where he intended to stay for good, thus enjoying Hina's charms from within. But soon Maui ejected him, and singing his own song, shrank and entered Te Tuna, tearing apart the monster's very flesh and sinew and killing him.

Stepping lightly out, Maui lopped off the monster's head and, at his mother's suggestion, planted it near the corner of his house. Peace and love-making resumed in the land of the wonder-workers, and one afternoon Maui noticed a green shoot growing from the place where Te Tuna's head had been buried.

Maui's mother explained that this was a tree that would bear a coconut with a sea-green husk and told her son to take care of it. When the tree grew and its fruit ripened, Maui plucked it. The coconut's meat was eaten by all, and everyone danced to celebrate how Maui had killed the Monster Eel and turned his head into food.

And that is how the people of this world came to have the coconut to eat.

Hera's Deceit

The whiff of revenge in this story adds a powerful frisson to Hera's sex-life and changes the destiny of kingdoms. Such love games are a hallmark of the tempestuous relationship of her marriage to Zeus.

The silence of fearfulness always made the tip of Hera's nose tingle. And that morning there was a chilly stillness in the air when she walked into Zeus' Olympian hall. That type of silence was a clear indication that Zeus had done something to arouse her anger and that the other gods knew this. She enjoyed their anxiety as they wondered how she would react.

Hera thrilled to the challenge. It was one of the exciting qualities of her marriage to Zeus.

She tipped up her chin as she surveyed the gods from the door of the hall, and lowered her eyelids so that her thick lashes concealed her eyes.

Zeus is tense, she noted with satisfaction.

She swept into the hall, seated herself on an ornate couch and glanced again at the faces of relatives, friends, admirers: concern mingled with anticipation. She arranged her robes around her, smoothed her hair, adjusted her girdle and refused to meet anyone's glance.

'I saw you on Mount Ida this morning,' she said at last, widening her eyes. 'You were with Thetis.'

Zeus began to bluster. 'What of it? I can speak with Thetis if I wish.'

'Is that all you were doing?' Hera's tone was silvery – she knew this musical quality in it made him squirm when he had reason to be guilty. 'She was sitting with her arms draped around your knees.'

'If you suggest that I was —'

'Did I say anything of the sort?' Hera raised her eyebrows. Squirm, Zeus, she thought. I love to see you squirm. For all your power and authority and strength, you squirm and wiggle under my words every time I want you to.

'What *are* you implying?' Zeus demanded.

'Well, we both know how Thetis is in these matters. She would —'

'Silence, Hera!' Zeus thundered.

'I was merely referring to the curse, Zeus.' Hera was gloating, though her tone pretended to soothe.

Poor Thetis! She had been forced to turn away both Zeus and Poseidon enthralled as they were with passion for her. How must she have felt to predict that the son she bore would one day be more powerful than his own father? Zeus and Poseidon had accepted the Nereid's rejection without protest. They had both witnessed the overthrow of their grandfather, Ouranos, by their father, Kronos. Then Zeus himself had destroyed Kronos. When a supreme god had to be overthrown, the bonds of love, the loyalty of wives, sisters, brothers, daughters, meant nothing. Zeus remembered well the machinations of his mother, Rhea, the strategies of his grandmother, Gaia, the Great Creatrix, the Twice

Destroyer, responsible for the downfall of two son-husbands.
Thetis had the same blood flowing through her veins: she,
too, could mother a destroyer.

Well, they had resolved the dilemma. They married Thetis
to a mortal, Peleus, King of Thessaly, and the child Achilles
had been born of the marriage. So Thetis may have been
deprived of bearing Zeus' seed, but there were enough
others who mothered his human progeny— Alcmene bore
him Heracles, Alcimede mothered Jason, and Danae
brought forth Perseus. And always the same explanation on
Zeus' lips when she caught him out: 'It is my duty as fertility
god. I am creator of humankind. The rulers of humankind
must carry the seed of divinity or what would differentiate
them from the common man?'

True – but his phallus throbbed at the sight of any young
female. Hera could only hope that all those human males he
had spawned would not be led by their flesh in the same
way as their divine father. Meanwhile she, Supreme
Goddess, must ensure that a balance was maintained in all
things. Of course she understood he had godly functions to
fulfil. So, too, did she: part of her purpose was to bring harmony, a task that had been entrusted to her since her
grandmother Gaia first created the cosmos.

Hera enjoyed the fireworks she contrived with Zeus. She
would reflect, as they lay together after they had battled
with thunderbolts and lightning showers, how conflict kept
alight the fire in their marriage. Thetis was no match for
her. But she knew what the Nereid was up to: she wanted
Zeus to support her son Achilles in the Trojan War. How
dare she interfere in matters of life and death? Wars, Zeus
believed, were the result of divine strategy. Their outcome

was for the gods to decide. As for the individuals striving in those battles, how could they be significant against a backdrop as inconceivably vast as that which the gods dealt with? If their feats made any impact on the cause, the gods would confer titles on them – hero, demi-god – they couldn't want more. How could Thetis intervene in a matter so important?

'What concerns me, my lord,' Hera continued, 'is that you never consult me before making your decisions. Thetis would not have been swathed around your legs if she had not wanted a favour.'

'My decisions are no concern of yours, Hera,' Zeus was blustering again, 'unless they're related to marriage and infidelity.'

Hera's hands flew to her cheeks. 'My lord! What a terrible thing to say! I'm a good wife and concerned with everything connected to you. Besides, the abduction of Helen by Paris was one of the reasons this war began and that is very much my business, you'll agree.'

She looked around the room for acquiescence, but all except Hephaestus dropped their eyes. He gazed pleadingly at her. As usual, Hera ignored her son. Hephaestus was a talented artisan, there was no doubt of that, but that was all. Bringing him up was one thing Thetis had been good for. Her own son Achilles would have gone up in a blaze, had not Peleus intervened in time. Well, that had spelled the end of *that* marriage.

'My alliances do not depend on your approval,' Zeus roared. 'Keep out of matters of war and peace.'

'I think,' she announced, 'that you have promised Thetis to help Achilles in this outrageous war. The sanctity of marriage may mean nothing to you, Zeus, but I have sworn to oppose Paris in his unholy intentions. I have a part to play here. What is Thetis' role?'

'So your interference stems from the trouble between Helen and Menelaus, does it?' Zeus glowered. 'Nothing, I imagine, to do with Paris choosing Aphrodite over you in the contest?'

'The contest?' Hera cocked her head on one side, playing with her necklace. 'I think not. A foolish game you played with Eris. The Judgement of Paris, they call it now. We goddesses only participated in the spirit of playfulness. But Paris has erred seriously this time. He has challenged the sanctity of marriage. And as for Thetis – or perhaps it is you I should hold responsible. Tell me, Zeus, how do you justify interfering in war because someone with power over your loins requests it?'

'If you continue to challenge me, Hera,' Zeus bellowed, rising, 'I will chastize you.'

'So!' Hera sprang to her feet. 'You give in to the pathetic pleadings of a Nereid even though it endangers the lives of many humans?'

Zeus raised his hand, and Hera ducked out of his reach. Hephaestus hobbled over to her.

'Mother, why make Zeus so angry for the sake of mortals? Reason with him. Calm him so that we can all be safe.'

Hera ignored the cup her son held out, so Hephaestus took her hands and moulded them around it. 'Take it, please,' he coaxed. 'Let the nectar cool your anger and soothe you.'

Hera smiled. She felt a surge of unusual affection for him as he limped around the seated gods, filling their goblets from the unending supply in his jug. She leaned back and murmured words of apology to Zeus. She would bide her time. Revenge would be the sweeter for being deferred.

That night when Zeus lay beside her, Hera watched him resentfully from the corner of her eye. She felt his fingers vibrate as he trailed them across the bare flesh of her arms. She would have pushed them away but indifference was a more powerful weapon. Breathing deeply, steadily, she let him think he had no effect on her. Zeus came closer, fitting his strong body along the length of hers, his penis erect and electric. But Hera was unresponsive.

The next day, as she watched him, far away on the highest peak of Mount Ida, overlooking the battle despite her opposition, she felt the same contempt. It was reprehensible of him to respond to Thetis but Thetis would learn that if she challenged Hera she would face defeat. Thetis had enjoyed Hera's protection as she grew up – was this the thanks she offered? And for Zeus to collude with the betrayal! But it was not Hera's way to harbour impotent grudges with all the discomfort and misery they brought. She preferred to take action. She would find a way to put things to rights.

Hera chuckled to herself. Revenge would contain the taste of honey and the scent of the rose, for beauty was one of the foremost weapons in her armoury. She had it in plenty, but her confidence and power increased when she lavished luxury on herself. Her dark eyes darted towards the doors of the chamber Hephaestus had built for her. She would lock them to avoid interruption. Then she would spend time thinking through each stage of her plan.

She cleansed her limbs with ambrosia, enjoying the soft sheen of her skin – heavenly to look at, sensuous to feel. The scent of the unguent was heady: one puff released in an

Olympian chamber would waft its way up to heaven and flutter down to earth. A warm rush of desire turned her thoughts to Zeus. How he loved to touch her skin. How she loved to feel him stroke it, and let his essence seep into her veins, flowing with the power of the intimacy they had shared forever – long before consciousness. Yes, she loved Zeus – yet how she hated him.

Oh! The ambivalence of love! The depth and breadth of emotions that tortured, taking over the mind and filling every breath with treacherous impulse. Yet that was the madness Hera craved: the struggle to claw back the power that love had wrested away. That was what she sought to ignite and fan into the leaping flames of passion. That was why their union was engorged with the energy, passion and vitality that made the cosmos whirl and swirl and burst into bloom.

The sheen of passion was on Hera's brow. She smoothed her ambrosial unguent from her palms into her hair, the luminous gold flowing like streams to her knees, and swiftly drew it up to the nape of her neck. Her laughter was soft and warm as a lover's breath as an errant lock tickled her skin. It reflected the sensation of Zeus' eyes on her neck, the tip of his tongue chasing an elusive wisp. He loved to disentangle her tresses, watch them disengage like golden snakes, slipping and gliding. Then he would let his lips slide down until they were pressed to the flesh of her thighs, and begin his quest for the gates to the temple of feminine mystery. Here he would anoint and caress, until he knew he had earned the right to enter and be initiated, her acolyte for an eternity of bliss.

In these moments of reverence she forgave him everything, letting the past incinerate in the heat of the passion from which every earthly seed sprouted and flourished. She would never harness Zeus, and as she revelled in the glory of union, she forgave also the future, celebrating the essence that was her lover. She could acknowledge that the urge which propelled him also prepared the way for other unions with her, where defeat became victory, where revenge turned into forgiveness, where thought and feeling were suspended in the stillness at the centre of time.

She surveyed herself in a pool of limpid crystal. She saw a perfect image, a matchless partner. 'All this in return for the defeat of a demi-mortal. For the price of a broken promise made to a Nereid.'

She shrugged her shoulders – the epitome of elegance. She tossed her head – the essence of wilfulness. Nothing consisted of a single intent: the ultimate goal was merely the culmination of a series of aims and events, each with its own sequences of complexity.

'Aphrodite,' she sang sweetly, 'I need you. Will you help me, little one?'

The impulsive, generous side of Aphrodite's nature could always be relied upon. Hera knew that.

'Queen of the gods, I am honoured. If it is a wish that may be fulfilled, then of course I will.'

Hera had listened carefully to Aphrodite's words. *If it is a wish that may be fulfilled*. Aphrodite was no fool: spontaneous and ready to give she may be, but she knew what she was doing. She was not, as many assumed, led by her passions, though no one would deny that she was dedicated to her principle, Love, and constant in its nurture.

If it is a wish that may be fulfilled. Hmm. Hera would have to resort to a little trickery. Oh, this was even more enjoyable than she had hoped! She had not intended to admit that she was seeking revenge on Zeus – Aphrodite might resist the use of Love for deception.

Hera sighed deeply, playing with the tips of her slender fingers, her eyes downcast. 'Oceanus and his wife Tethys have grown apart – the gulf between them is widening. I want to visit and end their conflict. I can reason with them, of course, and I will, but if they could make amends in their marriage bed, then how much easier my task will be. And that is where I need your help.'

'Ah, mighty protector of the sanctity of marriage!' Aphrodite laughed and Hera saluted herself: she had inserted just enough controversy into her request to make it appear genuine. Aphrodite, of all people being asked to help preserve fidelity? Well! If that wasn't at odds with her mission, what was?

'Love conquers all!' Aphrodite laughed. 'Even the dullness of the marriage bed. Yes, of course I will help you to bring Oceanus and Tethys back together in love and passion. But I don't promise to restrict them to each other.'

Hera drew her brows together in mild disapproval. 'Oh, Aphrodite!'

Aphrodite laughed again as her fingers undid a richly embroidered band from the bodice of her gown. 'In this panel are Love, Desire, Flirtation and Allure – enough to overwhelm anyone's senses. Take it and succeed in your noble mission.'

Hera grasped the band, laid it against her breast and fastened it on. 'How can I thank you, Little One?' she asked, her eyes filling with tears.

As soon as she was alone, Hera rose swiftly, made her

way to the door of her palace and stepped out. She pointed one delicate toe and arrived at Pieria, another footstep and she was in exquisite Emathia from where she crossed the snowy mountain summits of the Thracian horsemen, without her feet touching the ground, to Athos. From there she skimmed over the waves of the sea and arrived in the city of Lemnos. Her mission was to find Hypnos, Death's brother, and bend him to her will. It would not be easy, of course. Once before, when she had enlisted his help against Zeus, he had been badly singed.

Hera chuckled at the memory of her ruthlessness. Hypnos was a dreamy youth. It was as if he had inherited a portion of his mother's darkness to veil and shroud the dangers that might lurk behind hidden corners. Hera had exploited that haplessness before – when she had wanted one of Zeus' sons punished – and Hypnos, at her persuasion, had engulfed Zeus in his softness while the deed was done.

But Hypnos would remember Zeus' implacable fury and protest against her next request. Well, let him try: the past had always to be negotiated, it did not go away. Hera was ready with inducements to crumble Hypnos' resistance. She had made it her business to know all she could about Hypnos' passion. Titbits of gossip never passed her by – she stored them in the niches of her memory to be taken out when she needed them.

She flashed to his side, glowing, numinous, alluring. 'Dear Hypnos,' she whispered, 'I am in despair and you are the only one who can help me. If you do, I will always be grateful to you.'

Hypnos looked at Hera balefully, but before he could speak, she held up her fingers. 'Let me finish,' she continued, breathlessly. 'I am going to visit Zeus on Mount Ida where he has been seen consorting with Thetis. Imagine, a Nereid whom I myself brought up – to whom I entrusted my son. But I am going to win him back. Please help me.'

Hypnos flinched.

'Wait, Hypnos, hear me out. All I'm asking is that after Zeus and I have come together in love and passion, please lull him to sleep. Then, while he lies in my arms, I will know that he is still with me, not seeking another so soon after we've made love.'

Her voice was tremulous and she congratulated herself on the effect her words were clearly having on Hypnos.

'And it is not just eternal gratitude I offer you,' she coaxed. 'I will bring you a throne of gold, fashioned by Hephaestus, and a stool to rest your feet as you drink fine Olympian wine.'

Hypnos was tempted, she could see that. But fear was stronger than desire. 'Daughter of Kronos,' he begged, 'I would gladly send anyone to sleep, even mighty Oceanus and all his tributaries, to make you happy. But never again will I put Zeus to sleep unless it is by his own command.'

Hera pouted. 'How can you think that I would put you at such risk, Hypnos? You must think me heartless.'

Hypnos' limbs were heavy as he shifted position. 'Great goddess, you are asking me to violate Zeus' instructions. But I remember his divine rage the last time I put him to sleep at your behest. He would have me cast into the depths of Megara, to darkness and oblivion. I had to beg my mother to save me because no one wishes to displease Nyx, not even Zeus – but she would not help me twice for the same misdemeanour.'

'Trust me, Hypnos. I will protect you if Nyx will not.'

'Zeus only forgave me when I promised never to venture again into his aura unless he commanded me. I dare not offend him. Much as I wish to help you, Hera, I cannot risk being cast into the abyss.'

Hera had planned her response. She knew that Hypnos was hopelessly in love with a Grace, called Pasithea. 'My request – and it is only a request, dear Hypnos – springs from love and desire. How can it be ruthless? Love doesn't freeze and harden, it melts and softens.' She paused, and her eyelashes closed in a seductive curl. A tear glided to the tips and glistened, like a pearl nestling in a spray of sea-grass. She opened her eyes and studied her nails, each a pink petal. She was the picture of foresworn hope. But she sensed Hypnos weakening, felt his own unrequited love resonate with what he saw mirrored in her.

Hypnos made a gesture of helplessness. 'I feel for you, Hera,' he rumbled, 'but I have a function in the cosmos. I cannot risk Zeus' wrath again.'

Hera's eyes were imploring as she raised them to Hypnos. Her voice trembled like a fading melody.

'We are the same, you and I,' she murmured, 'tormented creatures . . . love eludes us.' She lowered her gaze. 'I know, you see, of your secret passion for Pasithea.' She raised her eyes to his, as if struck by a sudden thought.

'Would you agree if I were to promise you like for like? Zeus for me . . .' She let her words trail like scattered foam after the breaker's crash. 'No, of course not.'

Hypnos jerked himself upright. 'I don't understand. Do you mean . . .'

'Pasithea.' Hera's voice was dull. 'But of course not . . .

what's a reward if your life is threatened? I understand your fear.'

Hypnos could no longer contain himself. The image of Pasithea in his arms made him squirm. It made his juices flow. He was ready to risk all. One kiss from the lips of his beloved Pasithea would sustain him through an eternity of darkness in Tartarus.

He leaped to his feet. 'Let us go, Hera. In the name of Love, I'll risk all.'

Hera arose. 'In the name of Love,' she echoed with satisfaction.

She held out her arms and called the gentle mists of Lemnos to enfold her and Hypnos so that they could travel unseen over the ocean and across the land to Mount Ida. As they approached the tall forests on the crest of Ida, Hypnos paused to search out a hiding place among the trees until he found himself the highest fir on the mountain.

'This is where I will stay,' he said, 'or Zeus will see me.' Then he transformed himself into Chalcis, a flute-throated mountain bird.

Hera thanked Hypnos and bade him goodbye, then made her way to Gargarus, Zeus' favourite vantage-point which towered over the rest of Ida.

Zeus saw her coming. As she felt him glance in her direction, her heart leaped: his eyes contained the expression she had seen when they first made love, brother and sister, expressing their ardour in secret from Gaia and Kronos, their parents. That, too, had been on Mount Ida. She felt the thrill of the illicit as he moved forward, lust and longing glinting in his eyes. She rested her hand on Aphrodite's band. She held all the power.

'Hera, my sweet,' he whispered, 'how are you here without horse or chariot – as if you're visiting in secret?'

Hera pouted. 'You are accusing me of spying?'

Zeus held her close. 'You know I do not. And if you had found me with someone else, I would have dispatched her in a moment. Danaë, Alcmene, Leda, Semele – exquisite creatures, but nothing before you.'

His eyes softened. The silence embraced them. Zeus' breath caused the soft fabric of Hera's gown to stir, touch his skin, speak to him in the soundless words of sensation. Challenge sparked from her eyes in a gaze that said, 'I want you. Can you live up to my expectations?' But she said, 'I'm on my way to see Oceanus and Tethys. They lavished love on me once, now I want to repay it. You know their marriage is troubled?'

The gaze between them said, 'I desire you.'

'So why come to Ida? It is not on your way.' Zeus was in command for a moment. She allowed it, savouring the exchange of power.

'So that you would not complain that I wander to the edges of the earth without telling you.'

The gaze was still unwavering between them. Zeus moved forward, eyes still locked with hers, and enfolded her in his arms. Then he spoke. 'I have never desired you as I do now. I must make love to you.' He pulled her shoulder to his breast and dropped his head, kissing it roughly.

Hera pulled back, her hand flying to her lips. 'Zeus!'

He tightened his grasp on her. 'I know you feel the same.'

He was right. Despite her hidden reasons for seducing him, beyond her craving for revenge, lay the stirring urge to hold him close, so close they became fused together in a grand passion.

Hera's voice was barely a whisper. 'Everyone will see us. The supreme couple among the gods, couched together in the wilds of Ida, making unrestrained love. What if they gather to watch us, as if we were performers in the arena? Do we want them to laugh and mock as we all did when Hephaestus snared Aphrodite, strumping Ares? Why don't we go to our bedchamber where we can be alone?'

She felt Zeus harden against her. 'Now,' he insisted. 'Here. I'll draw a cloud around us.'

His hands were moving urgently, loosening her carefully coiled hair, letting it escape from the crown of her head down her shoulders and neck. His breath was coming in gasps yet his voice was still tender.

'I'll bring a cloud to surround us,' whispered the Cloud-gatherer. 'It will screen us from curious eyes.' He stroked her hair. 'A golden cloud, like your hair. We will be invisible even to the sun. So come, my sweet wife, hold back no longer.'

Hera had prolonged the ecstasy of anticipation as long as she could. Her heart was thudding. She had laid her plans well – they would see themselves through now. She would abandon herself to her eternal lover. She leaned her body against his. Slowly, he sank to the ground, holding her in his arms.

As they lay, Zeus' arms clasped around Hera's body, a lush, verdant carpet of new grass sprang up beneath them, lotus blossoms stirred into life, encrusted with dew-pearls, bulbs of crocus and hyacinth thrust forth their flowers, covering the ground with bursts of colour and life. And they

were draped about in a luminous cloud of gold, which produced a shower of glistening dewdrops.

These, then, were the moves and triumphs of the *hieros
gamos*, the sacred marriage, the divine game of love. And in
those moments of distraction and creation, did it matter that
a life Zeus had promised to protect slipped away without
cosmic consequence?

The Conception of Hatshepsut

Hatshepsut pulled off her complex stratagem with aston-
ishing finesse. In a clever move she established her divine
credentials, validated her claim to the throne – and gave
the world a fine ruler and a very sexy myth.

Amun-Re held his divine phallus; stroking its length, its firm,
sinewy width. The Ennead looked on in awe. This was the
source of their existence, though they had not witnessed the
great explosion that brought the world into existence, they
knew this was so. Amun had told them many a time.

'I first existed in the great Nowhere, the murky pond of
non-existence that was my Mother Nu, the primordial water.
I felt the urge. I knew I must create. I embraced my shadow-
image, I grasped my mighty phallus in my clenched hand
and had congress with it. I learned sensation and knew
ecstasy as I stroked and rubbed, my palms palpating, my
fingers flying along its length until, with the first explosion,
I created the world.

'From my emissions came Tefnut, who was moisture and
Shu, who was air. They bore Geb and Nut, Earth and Sky
from whom came the Splendid Lord Osiris and the
Magnificent Lady Isis and the other couple Set and

Nephthys. From Osiris' seed, the lady Isis bore Horus, the King eternal. I was aware when, through a deception, Nephthys conceived Anubis from Osiris. It was I who guided Isis in her search for that dog-child and filled her heart with such mercy for the child that she made him her own. I was the divine phallus of gold moulded by Isis and worn by Osiris into eternity. It was I who oversaw the battle for kingship between Set and Horus, I who issued the final decree in favour of Horus. It is I who reside in the body of every pharaoh who rules the Land of Egypt. I who appointed Osiris the Spirit of the Monarchy and Isis Protector of the Throne and Crown. And these are the members of the mighty Ennead.

'What a fine tool this is – this organ imprinted on the minds of my creation, the great phallus representing my might and power when painted on the bodies of the pharaohs. My phallus incarnate is seen on a hundred images, in the golden shape that Isis, the great enchantress, modelled. Now, after its great achievements, it rests, inactive, ineffectual, wanting a deed. But what is there left to create? Where is the pleasure of the climax when nothing is to come of it? So I've decided to create the one thing I have never made before. And this required careful thought because in producing this hitherto missing element I must also bring the female principle in balance with my male one. I have therefore decided to create a pharaoh who is a woman.'

When Amun-Re announced this decision to the Ennead, he met with an enquiring silence. Only Isis responded openly, jangling her sistrum, laughing in sheer delight. 'At last, Amun-Re,' she said, as the Creator-god looked at her quizzically. He knew Isis well enough now to understand that she could get the better of him whenever she chose, woman of magic that she was. The tensions between them were resolved but he would never forget how she had taken the form of a snake to discover his ineffable name, nor the time she had manipulated him in favour of Horus. Still, it had all fitted in with his great plan and all was well in his family. Amun-Re enjoyed Isis' approval. It made the others far more pliant.

Isis was dancing now, pirouetting past each of the other eight, smiling, teasing, enthusing them. 'I will watch over this woman-pharaoh,' she vowed. 'I'll bless her with the wisdom of the throne incarnate. I'll visit the gifts of song and music upon her. Her instincts will be as swift as those of the gazelle, her courage that of the pouncing tiger. And I'll give her patience – the patience of the woman searching for the fulfilment of her destiny. The patience of the wandering Isis. She will be my protégée in every way.'

Thoth, Knower of Knowledge and Giver of Wisdom, stepped forward. 'It is a worthy plan,' he said. 'This queen-pharaoh must be conceived direct from your body on Queen Ahmosis-Nefertary, sister-wife of the current good god-Pharaoh Thutmose. She is beautiful and noble, worthy of the god-seed. Your Majesty should visit her and implant in her womb the grace of the seed that has known no other form but yours. She awaits you in her bed.'

Ahmosis-Nefertary lay sleeping in her bed, loose-limbed and spread out like a blossom unfurling. Amun-Re breathed heavily at the sight of this woman of beauty who was to be his transient mate. He admired the transparent sheen on her skin brought by the balmy night. She moved slightly, easing herself on to her back, her arms flung out, her body vulnerable, the left ankle forming the base of a triangle with the right knee, its apex at the top of her thighs. It was a gesture of abandon, yet innocent. She sleeps, Amun-Re observed, the slumber of the young.

His eyes wandered over her body, her curving waist, the rounded, ivory belly, which rose and fell as she breathed. Her lashes flickered; her breasts, flattened and spread, still retained their roundness as they spilled out of the diaphanous fabric that clothed her body, and as Amun moved closer and his breath fell on her, her nipples grew firm, then blossomed.

In his excitement, Amun almost forgot that he was still in his divine form. He cast his eye on the Pharaoh lying in his magnificent bed in the adjacent room. This was a good man, a true son of Amun-Re, a worthy earthly protector for his child. He stretched himself above the sleeping Pharaoh and the next moment he was breathing within him. The Triad of Existence, expelled from Thutmose, clustered around him for a moment. Amun opened Thutmose's eyes, raised his body and went into it on his way to the bedchamber of Ahmosis. Then Ka, the secret twin, lay down to replace the one Amun had claimed. Smoothing the feathers of his ruffled bird-head, the soul, Ba, took position beside the tongue of flame that was the spirit, Khou; soul and spirit, side by side, hovered over Ka, awaiting the return of the body.

Amun-Re opened the silver-banded doors of cedarwood and paused a moment, gazing through Thutmose's eyes at Ahmosis. She was truly exquisite, truly a worthy mother for the great female she was about to conceive. And as he approached her bed, placed his hand on the lion head of one of its posts, his gleaming aura reflected off the walls and glass of her room and made her luminous.

Gently Amun reached out his hand, and stroked her cheek with his forefinger. A strand of hair had come loose by her temple and drifted to the side of her face like a reed-frond on a silver pond. Amun blew gently on it and it flickered back over her cheek, triggering a quirk of her mouth. Amun blew again. The hair frond tickled. The supreme god smiled through the lips of Thutmose. What a fortunate man to have a wife so beautiful. He was enjoying the ways of mortals. They made love differently. He knew only too well by now that, once triggered, the process of creation took on its own shapes and quirks. He could not hope to keep track of them all – neither did he care to. His attempt to control the ways of humans through the eye of Hathor had resulted once in disaster. Now he dealt with the metaphysics. The rest he left to others.

And this was the first time he had ventured into the phys-ical world of humankind. It was proving intensely pleasurable: he would take his time, learn their ways, savour the taste. He chased the wisp of hair with his tongue.

Ahmosis opened her eyes, looked into Amun's gazing at her through her husband's face. Amun was glowing in the dark but she was too sleepy to register that Thutmose did not usually shine. She touched his face lightly, then tucked both hands beneath her cheek and snuggled back into slum-ber. Amun drew close. The sap was rising inside him as he'd never known it before. For him the act of procreation was intentional, well judged, swiftly executed, a necessary act. But he was learning that it was different for mortals. There was a game to be played of extended pleasure coaxed from a slow, leisurely enjoyment, which brought all the human senses into play. There was a dance to be danced of changing rhythm and supremacy – in a measured instant, his to give, hers to refuse, hers to grant, his to accept. He would take his time – a god's time, infinite, vast and full – to explore all these human sensations of body and spirit. He would play the game and dance the dance, and savour the interplay of body with soul.

Amun looked long and close at the sleeping face of Ahmosis, then touched his nose to hers, dropping a kiss on her lips.

Ahmosis squirmed with pleasure, her mouth raised eagerly to retain the contact. Amun retreated, slowly, and Ahmosis moved forward with him, as if attached by a flimsy string of light. As he withdrew, Ahmosis awoke fully and sat up. Amun could see desire glittering in her eyes. He saw the swell of her breasts as she surged forward with yearning for him. He saw the peach flush on her cheeks as she called, her arms outstretched, 'Come to me, Thutmose. Lie beside me. Let me possess you.'

Amun could see his divine scent pervading her senses, overwhelming her as she fell back, her eyes dancing. In that moment he, too, experienced an intense longing. He wanted Ahmosis to love and desire *him* – not her brother-husband, not the man whose body he had stolen for a short while, but himself, the Supreme Creator, the Lord of the Ennead. The One and Only, the First One, without whom no one existed. And for her love, he would gladly forget it all. Amun's loins felt full and heavy. His heart was light and bright as it sang with feelings he had never imagined could exist.

Without further hesitation, he drew the veil from her eyes and showed himself to her in all his splendour and might. Her eyes darted over the jewels that adorned him – they were nothing to the eyes of a queen – to the twin plumes on his head.

Ahmosis swayed, as if she would faint. 'Lord Amun-Re!' she gasped.

Amun moved closer. His voice dropped, like that of any lover worried he may lose the desired one: 'Do you still crave me?'

He made himself motionless, still and silent, and wondered if her answer would bring him anguish. There were a dozen ways in which she might respond. She might protest fidelity to Thutmose. Or she might be terrified of divinity. Oh, what power she had in this moment! Did she know that she held the vulnerable heart of a mighty deity trembling in her delicate palm?

Ahmosis' gaze told Amun nothing. Neither did her smile, nor her soft laughter. Then at last, came the words: 'I desire you, Holy One. I am honoured by your visit.'

'It isn't honour I want from you Ahmosis. It is love. I have given you my heart.'

Ahmosis' eyes filled. Her fingertips dipped like a butterfly's wing into the reflecting tears in his own. They glistened on the balls of her fingers and as she looked at them she realized that this divinity, this greatest of all the gods, was begging a favour of her. 'I am delighted you are here,' she replied. 'I am overjoyed by your nearness, happy to feel you, so close and strong.'

'Ahmosis!' Amun-Re took her in his arms. 'Tell me more.'

'I welcome your body into mine,' Ahmosis continued. 'I have felt your presence beside me so often, from across the oceans of Being. But I have forced myself to be content with the knowledge of you, the presence of you, however remote.'

'I am here now. I am with you. Our love will always be praised.'

'Then don't wait,' whispered Ahmosis. 'Enter my body now. Infuse me with your magnificence. Water me with your divine dew.'

Gently Amun-Re, the mighty god, pushed Ahmosis back until she lay with her head on his arms. She raised her head and shoulders, pulled off one, then more of his magnificent jewels. Her boldness enchanted him and he lay still as she tugged at the symbols of his splendour and power, reducing him to nakedness.

'There,' she laughed and nipped his flesh playfully, 'you're unencumbered now. I will be your only ornament. I will wear you and you will wear me. Nothing will bar us from each other.'

He felt his nipples shrivel, then stiffen and become erect. She sighed deeply, then set upon him like a hungry child, licking, sucking until his every pore pulsated, alive and responsive. He lost count of the hours. What place had time in this tableau of bliss?

At last he rose and turned her over. Slowly he entered her, and she moved beneath him, reaching for him, guiding him in this exquisitely human ritual. The feel of her hands on his phallus sent strange jerks of pleasure through him. But he contained them, savouring her hands as they stroked his back, massaged his buttocks, scratched on the soft skin of his inner thighs, the obscure crevices of his tender and untouched places.

He caressed the soft skin of her face, her arms, her legs. And she matched his every gesture with passion until it was difficult to distinguish between their actions and overtures, where his began and hers took over.

He dropped soft kisses on her eyes, blew on her raven hair, nibbled her scented ear-lobes, breathing gently, tantalizingly into them. And every ecstatic moan that came from Ahmosis enhanced his excitement. This was no simple act of reproduction. This was the holiest act Amun-Re had ever experienced from the moment of that first contact with his own phallus. As his body was filled with the most exquisite of human sensations, he eased into a protracted, pulsing sea-rhythm, cradling and lapping Ahmosis, enfolding her in his movements until they were both surrounded by the great ocean that had divided them before and would divide them again.

In unison they sang out their jubilation. Then they wrapped their arms around each other and were silent for a long while. Finally, Amun-Re acknowledged that the time had come for him to go.

With a last close embrace, and a lingering kiss, he rose up and looked down tenderly at Ahmosis. 'I must leave you. But we have made a daughter who will grow up to be both wise and beautiful. She will rule over Upper and Lower Egypt and I will make the world peaceful for her. She will bring glory to your name and mine. And her name shall be Hatshepsut.'

Not so far in the future, when Hatshepsut became pharaoh, she ordered the story to be told in the paintings that adorned the temple she built to Amun-Re in Thebes.

And this was just as well because when Ahmosis awoke the morning after her intercourse with divinity she remembered nothing of Amun's visit.

But she was filled with a sense of well-being that she could not explain.

El

I'm both amused and amazed that the actor playing El had to hold up his penis on stage knowing he could face public rejection. Refusal might have resulted in seven years of drought and famine. Talk about risk!

This field is the field of gods
The field of Asherah and the Girl
They cook a kid in milk
A young goat in butter
The field of the gods
The field of Asherah and Rahmai
If the women cry 'Oh husband, husband!
Thy rod is lowered
The staff of thy hand has fallen'
While the bird roasts over the fire
Yea, broils over the coals,
Then the women are the wives of El
The wives of El and his forever.
But if the women cry 'Oh father, father!
Thy rod is lowered
The staff of thy hand has fallen'
While the bird roasts over the fire

Yea broils over the coals,
Then the women are the daughters of El
The daughters of El and his forever.
'Oh husband, husband!
Thy rod is lowered
The staff of thy hand has fallen'
While the bird roasts over the fire
Yea broils over the coals,
Then the women are the wives of El
The wives of El and his forever.
He bends their lips he kisses
Lo their lips are sweet, sweet as pomegranates.
From kissing, there is conception
From embracing, impregnation.
They go into labour and bear Dawn to Dusk.
Word was brought to El:
'El's wives have borne.'
'What have they borne?
My children, Dawn and Dusk.'
A lip to earth,
A lip to heaven
So that there enter their mouth
The fowl of heaven
And fish of the sea.
There ye shall sojourn among the stones and trees
Seven full years
E'en eight circling (years)
Till ye Good Gods walk the field
E'en tread the corners of the wilderness.'
They met the Guardian of the Sown
And shouted to the Guardian of the Sown:

'O Guardian, Guardian, open!'
And he opened an aperture for them so
    that they entered.

'If there is bread, give that we may eat.
If there is wine, give that we may drink.'

Aroma's Trick

Miss Aroma agrees to share her admirer with her less fortunate neighbour – but it's the poor man's reputation for virility that's at stake.

In the twilight hour when lamps were being kindled in the houses round about, the neighbor woman softly closed her house door and darted across the street under cover of darkness.

Aroma was in a waggish mood. 'What a pity,' she said, putting on the longest face she could manage.

'Nothing is going to happen after all. He has just sent a letter saying he could not come – an urgent appointment, a banquet he is absolutely obliged to attend. You may as well turn around and go home again.'

The neighbor woman listened with disappointment bordering on rage. Sparks flew from her eyes and steam spurted from her nose. She boiled inwardly. Why had Aroma not told her sooner? She would not have put herself to so much pains. Suspicion was born in her heart: no doubt Aroma had regretted her promise. She had decided that her friend would only be in the way, that she preferred to keep the night's pleasures all to herself. The neighbor woman was working herself up into a resounding tantrum when Aroma's merry laughter dispelled the clouds.

'Fooled you! How can you be so gullible! I just wanted to tease you a little. Set your mind at rest. He will come. Quickly, now, we must get ready.'

She led her friend into the kitchen. There they set a kettle full of fresh water over the hearth fire and prepared a warm hip bath in a large tub. Returning to the bedroom, they moved an upholstered love seat close to the foot end of the bed. Here Aroma planned to make herself comfortable and play the eavesdropper during the first part of the night. Then she sent her friend out to listen behind the outer gate of the house.

'Bolt the door and wait until he comes. He is sure to make his presence known by knocking softly. At the very first knock pull the bolt and let him in. Don't give him time to repeat his knocking or knock more loudly; the sound might be heard in the neighborhood and arouse suspicion. As soon as you have let him in, bolt the door again. And one thing more: when you return to the room and get into bed with him, speak as little as possible. If he asks you questions and you can't help answering, do it in a whisper. Don't give yourself away by your voice, or our whole stratagem will be ruined.'

The neighbor woman promised to follow her instructions to the letter and repaired to her listening post behind the outer door, while Aroma put out all the lights in the house and settled down on the love seat.

A whole hour passed. The neighbor woman came in again, footsore from standing there and unnerved from listening: no one had knocked. She was just opening her mouth to report to Aroma when suddenly someone embraced her and kissed her in the darkness. First she thought it was Aroma. Another of her jokes, no doubt. To make sure, she let her hand slip down along the someone's body. Lo and behold, she encountered something long and hard – a he!

'Dearest!' she whispered, fighting back her impulse to cry aloud. 'Oh, oh, however did you get in?'

'Over the rooftops.'

'Oh, what a wonderful man! Come, let's go to bed.'

They undressed. But though far from reluctant, he could not keep pace with her. She was lying stark naked on her back while he was still removing his clothes. At last he had finished. He climbed in, lay down on top of her, and groped for her legs, meaning to toss them over his shoulders as usual. But his hands met with the void. She had already raised her legs and spread them wide. She had prepared an eager welcome for him.

'She certainly comes straight to the point,' he said to himself. 'Well, so much the better. There will be no need to waste my time beating around the bush. I, too, shall come straight to the point.' And he poised his battle-axe for a frontal attack. But she had not been prepared for so violent an onslaught. What a vigorous warrior was storming at her gate and demanding admittance! And she began to squeak and struggle.

'*Hach . . . bh!* Take it easy. You are hurting me,' she pleaded, gasping for air.

Gentleman as he was, he granted her a respite which he utilized to finger her portal, gently parting the wings of her gateway and rubbing persistently this way and that. Then he attacked again. But again he failed to breach the fortress.

The head of his tortoise squeezed in an inch or so, while the van of his army was repulsed.

'There is nothing to be gained by pussyfooting,' he explained to her. 'The best strategy is an all-out offensive. It may hurt you at first, but if you can stand it, your pleasure will be all the greater afterward.'

And he attacked vigorously. But again she struggled and resisted.

'*Shih pu-te!* It won't work that way. Please, a little saliva would help.'

'Certainly not. That is contrary to all the rules of the game. That may be permissible when there's a maidenhead to be pierced, but not otherwise.' He attempted another assault, but her resistance was undiminished.

'*Shih pu-te!* It can't be done. If you are too proud to break the rules, I'll attend to it.'

She struggled loose, spat in the hollow of her hand, and used one half of the saliva to lubricate her gate, the other half to anoint the head and neck of his tortoise.

'It will be better now. But gently, please.'

He disregarded her plea. On the contrary, he wished to show her what he could do. Clutching her hind cheeks firmly and pulling her to him so brusquely that flesh met flesh with a loud report, he attacked with all his might. This time he broke through, successfully introducing his entire armament into the fortress.

She uttered a soft scream, this time less from pain than from admiration.

'Goodness! Who would have expected a young scholar like you, a stay-at-home bookworm, to be so mighty a warrior! He doesn't even care whether his victim lives or dies. He just pushes his way in and that's that. You've reached rock bottom, you can't get any further. So out with you, and make it quick!'

'Oho! We're just beginning. A fine how-do-you-do if I were to retire from business now,' he replied with a merry laugh, and began to heave and thrash with all his might and main. At first each of his thrusts brought forth a moan: '*hach . . . bh.*' After fifty odd strokes she fell silent. After he had passed the hundred mark, she began to moan again: the same sounds of '*hach . . . bh . . .*' issued from her lips. At first her moaning had been from pain, but now it signified rapture. It is, indeed, a strange fact that women can express very different feelings with the same sound: first it is a sound of suffering and then it becomes a sound of pleasure. With her pleasure moan a woman makes it known that her ecstasy is approaching the peak, that the cloud over the magic mountain is close to bursting.

Now Aroma's neighbor exerted all her guile and cunning. Her cloud had already burst twice, but when our young man asked her if she had come to the point, she said no and insisted that he persevere in his efforts. Why did she lie? Because she knew that she was only Aroma's substitute and that Aroma was listening. If she admitted that her joys had come to a head, Aroma would step in and take her place She wished to enjoy the rare pleasures of this night to the full, to prolong them as much as possible. She observed the well-known practice of the substitute officials described in the popular saying:

> *These worthy gentlemen are substitutes in office:*
> *Slowly does it, take your time.*
> *The public may be good and sick of waiting their turn.*
> *What matter! Meanwhile we draw our wages.*

In this love battle there was a certain amount of cheating on both sides. She cheated in defense of her interests. He for his part cheated in defense of his prestige. When in answer to his question she kept saying no, she had not yet come to the point, he felt himself in honor bound to give the same untruthful answer to the same question, and to continue bravely in his efforts. He didn't want her to be disappointed in him, though by now he was hard pressed and would have welcomed a breathing spell. In this phase of the battle, he was very much like a drunken man riding a donkey, his head tottering alarmingly at every step.

She must have noticed the difference between the easy spontaneous vigor with which he had started out and his present convulsive effort. Taking pity on him, she asked:

'Dearest, have you come to the point?'

And still his pride would not let him give in. Her question produced the same effect as the scolding with which a master shakes up a sleepy pupil and spurs him to new wakefulness. He redoubled his exertions and struggled bravely on. But when he began to sweat and pant, she relented.

'*Wo tiu la!* I've done it. Stop. I can't go on. I am dying. Put your arms around me and let us go to sleep side by side.'

With these words she offered him the armistice for which he had been secretly longing. He was only too glad to accept.

Meanwhile Aroma had played the eavesdropper. The whole time she had lain motionless on the love seat at the foot end of the bed, listening intently.

In the beginning, when the neighbor woman had squeaked and struggled and his attack seemed to be making no progress, she had said to herself, Well, his utensil can hardly be so insignificant; it must indeed be quite imposing and serviceable. Already half her doubts were dispelled. And as the battle progressed, when she saw, or rather heard, how perseveringly he held up his end and how, after a brief moment of weariness, he rallied his flagging troops and led them back into the fray with redoubled vigor, she was wholly reassured. 'He is a born conqueror of ladies' chambers, my chosen hero,' she said to herself. 'I shall belong to him with joy and without regret.'

Taking advantage of the deep sleep into which the couple had fallen, she slipped quietly off the love seat. For a time she stood in the dark and pondered. She might slip unnoticed under the covers and simply join in when the couple woke up. But in the darkness, she told herself, he would be unable to distinguish her from her neighbour: what was to prevent him from devoting his attentions to the neighbor woman? That simply wouldn't do. Or even if he should turn to Aroma, he would not perceive her beauty in the darkness. That would be depriving him of just what he needed to rekindle his passion and fire him on to new deeds. He had every right to be tired, and without the proper inspiration he would provide her with nothing but cold and savorless leftovers. No, that was not at all what she wanted. She would proceed in a very different way.

She slipped secretly into the kitchen, where she poured several ladles full of water into a kettle which she set on the hearth fire. Then she kindled a straw in the fire and lit a lamp. Lamp in hand, she returned to the bedroom, approached the bed and lifted the curtain. She removed the silk coverlet from the sleeping pair, shone the lamp in their face, and burst out in simulated rage:

'Heigh, what kind of behavior is this? Breaking into strange houses in the middle of the night and lying around in other people's beds! Up with you! Give an account of yourself!'

Our scholar gave a violent start. Drowsy and befuddled as he was, he mistook the intruder for the irate husband: no doubt he had been hiding in the house the whole while, waiting to catch his wife's lover in the act with a view to blackmail. For a moment our scholar was scared to death and a cold sweat poured down his back, but soon he gathered his wits, and when he looked up he saw none other than the object of his adoration standing before him in the lamplight. He rubbed his eyes. How was it possible? Why, he had just been sleeping with her – or did she have a double? He turned his head and looked at the woman by his side. Now, in the glow of the lamp, he distinguished her features for the first time and started back in horror. That blackened skin riddled with pockmarks! That flat nose, that broad mouth! That strawlike, lusterless hair! His eyes moved downward along her body. It was shapely enough, but here too her skin was covered with spots.

'Who are you?' he asked.

'I am the neighbor from across the street. At Madame Aroma's express request I took her place just this once. She wanted me to test you. It all began that first day when you were walking up and down in front of the shop . . .' With disarming simplicity she revealed the whole truth from A to Z.

She climbed out of the bed and quickly slipped into her things, though in her haste she put on only what was strictly necessary: her lined trousers, her padded cotton jacket, her felt slippers. All the rest – stockings, underwear, tunic, sweat cloth – she gathered into a bundle which she tossed over her arm. At the door she turned back:

'Plain as I am,' she said, 'I shall for ever be your humble servant. It was as a favor to my friend that I shared your couch tonight, but perhaps we were predestined from an earlier existence to lie together. Who knows? If ever you should come again and have a few minutes to spare for me, your devoted handmaiden will always be at your disposal. Do not treat her too unkindly.'

She bowed to him and then to Aroma, muttered a few words of thanks for the friendly reception, and departed. Aroma accompanied her to the house door, let her out and barred the door behind her.

When she returned, our young man was still quite bewildered. He felt as though he had just awakened from a deep dream or a drunken stupor.

'Well,' said Aroma, with an affectation of coldness, 'why are you still lying here? The other has settled accounts for me. We are quits. You have had your pleasure. Why don't you go home?'

He protested vigorously. 'Oho, we are far from being quits. Quite on the contrary. You owe me reparation for the injustice you have done me by defrauding me with so inferior a substitute. It is midnight already, soon it will be dawn. We have no time to lose. Quickly. Crawl in here beside me, and not another word!'

'Do you really mean it?'

'I certainly do.'

'Very well. In that case, you will kindly get up and dress? Before we go to bed, there is something important to be done.'

'What can be so important? As far as I can see, the one important thing is that we go to bed together.'

'Stop asking questions and come along.'

He jumped up and flung on his clothes. Taking him by the hand, she led him through several rooms and inner court-yards to the kitchen. There she pointed to the bathtub and the kettle full of boiling hot water on the hearth fire. Now he understood. He was to take a bath, and since it was far to the kitchen and the way led through open courtyards, she had bidden him dress, fearing that he might catch cold if exposed to the cool night air. How considerate of her! In his thoughts he performed a kowtow of thanks.

Meanwhile she plied the ladle and filled the tub half with cold, half with hot water. The result was a fine warm bath, not too hot and not too cold.

'There. Now you can get in. You will find soap and wash-cloths over there. Help yourself.'

And she continued:

'An unsavory smell of strange woman still clings to you. I should not like you to pass it on to my sensitive body.'

'You are perfectly right,' he agreed. 'It is indeed of the utmost importance. I shall also wash my mouth out to oblit-erate every trace of kisses.'

And he reached for the water bowl and the toothbrush which had been placed in a rack affixed to the outside of the bathtub. He was very much impressed to note that despite the late romantic hour she was still the perfect housewife, attentive to every imaginable domestic detail. How carefully she had prepared his bath, complete with soap, washcloths and steaming warm towels! When he had finished drying himself, she had wiped off the wet bath mat with a rag, and later on in the bedchamber she had prepared a sweat cloth and placed it in readiness beside the pillow.

What an excellent housekeeper! he thought in silent admiration. She thinks of everything.

She put out the lamp and sat down on the edge of the bed. Slowly she undressed, carefully smoothing out each garment and folding it over a chair.

Graciously she let her lover finish undressing her, loosen her silk brassière and remove her thin batiste panties. He embraced her and kissed her and sent out a hand to explore. He found her twin hills, so full and elastic that they slipped out of his hands when he tried to pull and pluck at them. Everywhere her flesh was firm, but at the same time it was soft and tender; nowhere did he find a hard place. Further down, on the vault of her fortress wall, he met with the same soft firmness, but here the skin seemed to be even smoother and more supple than elsewhere.

He moved her carefully into place, raised her legs over his shoulders, and opened the battle, employing the same tactics as with her ugly precursor; a frontal attack without introductory love play. His calculation was that though this approach might hurt her at first, her pleasure would be all the greater afterwards. The offensive ran off without a hitch. But contrary to his expectations, she remained utterly apathetic as though she felt nothing at all, giving no sign either of pleasure or of pain. Then he remembered what his experienced friend, K'un-lun's Rival, had told him about the mighty caliber of her husband's last. No wonder his forces had been able to slip into the enemy fortress so easily, without encountering the least resistance. He had not been prepared for a shoe of such dimensions. In a shoe so deep and wide his last, though by no means unimpressive, seemed to shrivel into nothingness, to lose itself like a needle in a haystack.

Aware that he would get nowhere by the old methods, he decided on a change of tactics. Removing the pillow from under Aroma's head, he pushed it beneath her loins. In so doing, he intentionally neglected to provide her head with another support. This impressed her and inspired her with a secret admiration. Thus far she had experienced no pleasure at all, but she saw by his preparations that he knew a thing or two about bedchamber technique and was confident that everything would come out all right in the end.

Esteemed reader, the battle of the sexes is in many respects not unlike the art of warfare: before the opening of hostilities, the two contestants spy upon each other, feeling out one another's strengths and weaknesses. He tries to find out whether she is deep or not so deep, in order to plan his offensive and retreat accordingly. She tries to obtain accurate information about his armament, whether short or long, thick or thin, in order to meet it with suitable movements and adapt herself to it. Success in battle depends on knowledge of the enemy's strength or weakness. The length and thickness of men's utensils vary exceedingly, and the same applies to the depth and width of women's pleasure houses. If she is not particularly deep, an over-long utensil is out of place; there will not be room for it, at least not for all of it. If he should nevertheless attempt to force the whole of it in, he will give her not pleasure but pain. Ought he to get all the pleasure? That would be unfair. But if she possesses an extraordinarily deep pleasure grotto, she needs a mate with unusually long and powerful armament; otherwise she will get no satisfaction. But the length of the male organ is fixed by nature once and for all; it does not go on growing and there is no way of lengthening it artificially. Consequently a knowing lover resorts to a stratagem: he removes the pillow from beneath his lady's head and wedges it under her waist. Thus raised, her pelvis lies flatter and the lover's utensil is so enabled to reach the bottom. This should not be taken to mean that the pillow beneath the waist is indispensable or should be employed in every case. It is indicated only in cases when the lady's pleasure grotto is too deep for her lover's armament. We see then that this shortcoming can be remedied. But there is another discrepancy that cannot be made good: when the lady's shoe is too wide for her lover's last.

The itinerant surgeon's operation had considerably increased the thickness and stamina of our young man's equipment, but had not lengthened it. On his first attempt to penetrate Aroma's pleasure grotto, his utensil had proved too short and had failed to plumb the depths. By hitting on the above-mentioned stratagem of wedging the pillow under her waist, he had impressed her with his competence; she said nothing but secretly she was very pleased.

This use of a pillow is a simple and widely known trick, but few men are considerate enough to bother and still fewer know how to do the thing properly. In addition to supporting the waist, most men leave the pillow under their lady's head. This is a big mistake. For her body is then raised at both ends, with the result that she is bent in the middle. If, to make matters worse, her lover rests his whole weight upon her, it is easy to imagine how uncomfortable she must feel. In this unnatural position, a kiss requires the most painful contortions on both sides: *he* must hump his back in order to reach her mouth; *she* must stretch her neck and twist her head backward before her lips and tongue can meet his lips and tongue. All this because of the troublesome and superfluous pillow under her head. And so I say, away with it! Let the lady's cloud-coiffure lie directly on the sheet. Then the heads and limbs of both parties will fit harmoniously together; his noble yak whisk will penetrate her pleasure grotto without difficulty, her purple little tongue will find its way easily into his mouth, no inequalities of position will prevent them from merging and blending inwardly, no discomfort will mar their pleasure.

After this brief digression, let us get on with our story. Raising her nephrite thighs over his shoulders, planting both hands on the bed sheet, our scholar resumed the interrupted battle – this time with success. His valiant henchman did not bely his partly canine origins and nature. The longer the battle raged, the more imposing became his stature and with it his courage; no longer was her pleasure grotto a bottomless pit; both on the sides and in the depths the desired contact was established. Aroma's attitude changed accordingly. The first assault had left her totally apathetic and inert, no sound of pleasure or pain had escaped her; but now her body began to quiver and writhe voluptuously, and moans of *'hach . . . bh . . .'* issued from her lips.

'*Hsin-kan*, dearest. It's coming! I feel a pleasant sensation.'

'So soon? Why, I've hardly begun,' he whispered back. 'Just wait until I get going, then you will really feel something, *wo-ti kuai jou*, my perverse little lump of flesh.' And he proceeded to heave and thrash until heaven and earth were stricken with terror and threatened to lose their balance. Her stifled cries of 'Dearest' and 'Oh, I'm dying' became more and more frequent and the grass and bushes round her gate grew moist with the dew of pleasure. He reached for the sweat cloth to wipe away the dew, but she restrained him. How so? It has already been stated that she was very passionate by nature. A battle of the sexes, she felt, should be a wild frenzy, an ecstatic temple dance with a rousing accompaniment of gongs and drums. Interrupt the temple dance with a prosaic sweat cloth? Out of the question. Even in her everyday dealings with her husband she had taken the same attitude. Let the dew of pleasure sprinkle her as it might, there would be no wiping until afterward, after the cloud had burst. This was a very personal eccentricity of hers. I mention it only in passing and – it goes without saying – only for the benefit of gourmets and connoisseurs!

Our young man was still going strong when she flung her arms round his neck, pressed him close, and groaned: '*Wo yao tiu la!* My cloud is bursting. Let us die of joy together.'

Actually it was too soon for him. He would have been glad to go on a little longer and impress her with his vigor and endurance. But she would not allow it.

'Stop. I am fully convinced of your strength and endurance. You've been battling all through the night, you've taken on two women and laid them low. Grant yourself a little rest, save your strength for tomorrow night; I shouldn't like you to get sick from over-exertion; I want you to stay well for my sake.'

Ah, she was concerned for his health. How considerate! How touching! Deeply moved, he folded her in his arms, pressed her tight, and body to body, they shared the ineffable bliss of the bursting cloud.

The Lusty Lass

I thoroughly enjoyed this saucy country-girl's bold attempts to lose her virginity. The despair of missing out on sexual experience is obviously timeless.

As I was walking in the woods this year
I met a lusty lass.
She did ask me straightaway,
'Tell me kindly, what is your errand?
Under green branches
will you come to sit close by me?'

I answered the beauty of flowers' hue,
'I'm pretty poor at conversation.
In a secluded place bashful modesty
quite overwhelms me,
and with that
I'm of no use to amuse you.'

'Listen to the complaint of a lovely lass
whose land is missing its season,
and I am afraid of wetness,

and indeed I'm without succour.
I'm in a bad state
in need of a ploughman for this land.'

I answered my fine maid,
'I'm not used to ploughing either.
I can't weave my plough in and out very well,
my sweet maid, by night or morning,
nor guide its thrusts
to part the two sods as it should.'

'If that's all that's troubling you
there's no need at all for you to hesitate.
If your ploughshare is inclined to the furrow,
It'll make no sound under the burdock,
there's a perfectly good way,
you call [the oxen], and I'll hold [the plough].'

'My ploughshare, if you'll believe me sweetheart,
is a mere flake which hasn't yet hardened,
and I'm a backward lad
in desire to thrust towards your earth,
to sport with you as a mate,
for fear that you play dirty, lass.'

'Farewell then, I give up,
woe is me that I was ever born and raised.
None of the boys will help me out
between my knees despite their beauty.
There's no doubt that I was born
under an unlucky grievous star.'

Dahama and Moussa

Dahama

*Brief but pithy, this story follows a passage on the impor-
tance of kissing well. But the sting in the tale is, if you
can't follow kisses with coitus, you're in the dock.
Literally.*

It is related that Dahama ben Mesejel complained before
the governor of the province of Yamama that her husband,
El Ajaje, was impotent and neither cohabited with her nor
approached her. Her father, who assisted her in the case,
was blamed by the people of Yamama for this, and they
asked him if he was not ashamed to demand coition for his
daughter.

'I want her to have some children,' replied he; 'if she loses
them, God will hold her to account; if she keeps them, they
will be useful.'

Dahama presented her case in these words to the emir:

'Here is my husband; up to now he has left me intact.'

'You are perhaps unwilling,' objected the emir.

'On the contrary, I willingly lie down and open my
legs.'

'Oh, Emir, she lies! If I want to possess her I have to fight
hard,' exclaimed her husband.

'I will give you a year in which to prove the falsity of the allegation,' replied the emir to him. This he did, however, out of sympathy for the man.

El Ajaje then withdrew.

As soon as he got back home he took his wife in his arms and began to caress her and kiss her on the mouth; but that was the limit of his efforts, for he could give no proof of his virility. Dahama said to him: 'Cease your caresses and embraces; they do not suffice for love. What I need is a strong and rigid member whose sperm will flood my womb.'

In despair, El Ajaje took her back to her family and repudiated her that very night.

Know then that if a woman is to be satisfied, kisses without coition will not suffice. Her sole delight is in the penis, and she gives her love to the man who can use it well however disagreeable and deformed he is.

Moussa

Power, beauty, riches, all bow before the skills of a proficient lover. Another of Burton's translations from The Perfumed Garden, *which had me in stitches.*

It is related that Moussa ben Mesab went one day to the house of a lady who owned a female slave, a beautiful singer, to see if he could buy her. Now this lady was a great beauty and very rich. When he entered the house he noticed a man, still young but very deformed, who was giving orders. He enquired of the lady who the man was, and she replied:

'That is my husband, and I would willingly die for him.'

'You are reduced to a hard slavery, and I pity you; but we belong to God and shall return to Him! Still, what a calamity that such incomparable beauty and such a figure should belong to that man!'

'Oh, son, if he did to you behind what he does to me in front, you would sell all your goods and even your patrimony. You would then think him handsome, and his ugliness would change to perfection.'

'May God preserve him for you!' exclaimed Moussa.

Daghda's Love Trail

The annual union of Daghda, the promiscuous sky-father of the Celts, and the war-like Morrigan across the Unshin was well known. Daghda's technique certainly got the women on his side.

The woman saw clear across the horizon to the north of Ireland. Daghda had a tryst with her today, the day of the All Hallows battle. They would meet here not far south of his home where the river Unshin roars its way through Connacht. She watched as he stretched himself to his full, massive height, slung one club over his shoulder letting it drag behind him. The other club hung, large and half cocked in the front. It never lay down flat, that lusty organ, but now Daghda looked smug, no doubt at the thought that he was to meet her – the Morrigan, people called her – and that had put extra life into it. Today it bobbed roguishly ahead of him as he strode along.

He saw her from a great distance, as she stood astride the Unshin, one foot planted firmly to the north of the water, the other to the south. Nine wild tresses of hair had worked loose and flew like cloud streamers across the skyline. Ah, she was magnificent. He had hardly time to come up beside and behind her when his phallus grew to its full length, hardened and reared up in excited determination.

There was no need for words beyond a greeting. Morrigan was ready for him and they moved, gloriously smooth, as the waves of the Unshin lapped against their toes in a creative dance, now gushing, now whirling, now rising, now falling, breath on breath, thrust on thrust. Then it turned white and was swirling to a central vortex, sucked all life into itself, spinning it, wringing it and spewing it out in a massive regurgitation that soared on a white-crested surge and at last looped slowly down, throbbing, once, twice, three times, slow and long. Finally, the water resumed its normal rhythm and flow. And for that annual union of the divine pair, the Unshin got its name as the Bed of the Couple.

Deep from within her satisfaction, Morrigan spoke to Daghda. 'For the pleasure you've brought me, I will help you in your war against Indec mac De Domnann, the king of the Fomoire. I will take the blood of his heart and the kidneys of his valor. And I will destroy him.'

Soon all Ireland was in motion preparing for the second battle of Moy Tirra when the men of Ireland would take on the Fomoire. And Daghda decided he would visit the Fomorian camp and ask for a truce. That would delay them, buy time for his men of Ireland, and while he was there he would look around a little, try to discover what he could that might aid him in his fight.

The Fomoire accepted his truce and invited him to a meal with smiles that went no further than their lips and were put there by deceit. The massive appetite of this father of gods was well known and Indec, their king, ordered his royal cauldron to be filled with milk and fat, and goats, swine and sheep, to enrich the porridge to be prepared for Daghda. As they cooked, the Fomoire laughed and jeered at the thought of a single creature with the capacity to devour this quantity of food and they made bets among themselves – would Daghda indeed manage to consume all the food in this cauldron or would he give up half-way through? If he did they would not think less of him – indeed they might think more because this was food enough for an army. When the porridge was ready, they poured it into a huge hole in the ground. Then Indec, their king, invited Daghda to eat. 'If you do not finish every last bit of this food,' Indec told him, 'It will mean that you scoff at our hospitality and scorn our food. For that I will have to kill you.'

Daghda lifted the ladle, large enough for a man and a woman to lie in, and began to eat. Into his mouth with the first spoonful went halves of salted pig and a quarter of lard. Daghda praised the taste and quality of the food as he ladled it down his throat. When the porridge was all but finished and the ladle could scoop no more, he reached into the ditch with his hand and scraped up the residue by crooking his finger. Then he stroked his distended belly and released a stream of belches, large and small, stretched himself out and fell asleep.

Around him, the Fomorians beat their thighs and laughed, making a mockery of the huge god, his formidable appetite and the hillock that rose and fell around his middle as he breathed the long, deep breaths of slumber. But what did they know of the future, of their imminent plight and of the pledge of the Morrigan, great battle crow, goddess supreme?

When he had rested Daghda heaved himself up and made his way out of the camp. He had to drag himself along and sometimes he supported his belly with his huge arms. The Fomorians judged him, as no doubt did others, by the cloak that was so shrunken and small that it didn't even reach as far down as his elbows. Or the tunic of non-specific hue, dull and grubby, that floated just short of his buttocks, exposing his rear to the winds. Or his long phallus that stood proud of any covering ready to take on all challenges of love or war.

And challenges there were many. Even at this moment there was war brewing behind him in the Fomorian camp, and in front of him, a Fomorian girl appeared from nowhere. The Daghda took in her bright face, her supple figure, her lustrous tresses of hair, and he desired her. But the mound of his belly was a block separating his penis from his goal. The long organ remained tame and flaccid between his legs as if in terror of the hill above.

'Oho!' taunted the girl, 'You haven't much life in you, now, have you?'

'Out of my way, woman. I have important things to do.'

As Daghda brushed past her to continue on his way, the Fomorian girl leaped on him with a shout of protest. 'And who do you think you are, pushing me aside like that?' Without another word, she let out a loud battle-cry and hurled him to the ground.

He fell hard, thumping the tender part of his rear and the weight of his body caused a ditch to form beneath him. 'Take care not to offend me, girl,' Daghda warned angrily. 'What right have you to push me off my path?'

'The right to make you carry me on your back to my father's house.'

'Who is your father?'

'Indec, King of the Fomoire,' she said, flying at him again, punching and beating with such might that the excess from Daghda's belly was forced out, filling the ditch in which he sat. 'Now, will you agree to carry me home?'

'Not unless you call me by my name for I am under a curse that prevents me carrying anyone on my back unless they say my name in full.'

'Then tell me your name.'

Daghda's body felt lighter now and his wits brighter. He teased the girl for a while, giving her parts of his name, then refusing to obey her command because she had not fulfilled the conditions of the taboo and said all of it. Eventually, when he had enjoyed her increasing impatience to the full, he told her all of his names, which came to no less than twenty-eight. The Fomorian woman gazed at him in amazement.

'Too much to handle?' Daghda asked. 'Perhaps, then, you will not try to mock me any more.'

Slowly, he disengaged himself from the mess in the ditch and hoisted the woman on his back. The girl wanted him to move faster. She leaned back and struck him on his rear and as she did so, the front of her garment fell open – and there, for the Daghda to see, was a bush of coiling pubic hair. This time there was no impediment to his desire. He turned and slid her into his arms and did what he knew best how to do. Together they heaved and pulled, scratched and bit, wrestled and soothed to their full satisfaction.

At the end of their revels, the woman commanded Daghda not to go to war with the Fomorians, her people.

'Certainly I will go,' Daghda replied.

'Then I will be the stone at the mouth of every ford you cross,' she retorted.

'True, but I will tread on every stone and scar it for ever with my heel.'

'Then I will be a giant oak in every ford and in every pass you approach.'

'And I will pass you, marking every oak for ever with my axe.'

Suddenly the woman succumbed. 'Then let the Fomoire enter your land and I myself will sing spells and use the deadly art of the wand against them and that way you and the men of Ireland will win the war.'

From across the waves of the Unshin, the Morrigan, war-hag, laughed loudly. Her laughter streamed across Ireland. She recognized the pleasure-urge that had transformed the Fomorian woman from scornful enemy to pleading mistress. Oh that promiscuous old devil, that greedy old man: when it came to pleasuring women, there was none better than Daghda. He did it every time.

The Man of Quality

I

*Jim Colville's modern translations are robust and full,
like the Arabic original. I wonder if women – maybe the
Sultan's concubines – got their hands on them?*

One of the stimulants to sexual desire is the use of perfume by both partners. When a woman detects the scent of perfume on a man, she relaxes and unwinds. A man might thus try perfume as a means to coupling with a woman.

With this in mind, let us relate a story about Musaylima ibn Qays – may God curse him – the liar who claimed prophecy in the time of the true Prophet – may God bless him – and a band of perfidious Bedouin – may God damn them all!

This Musaylima used to produce his own fake and distorted versions of Quranic verses. A gang of hypocrites and dissenters once brought him the chapter of the Quran entitled 'The Elephant', revealed to the Prophet Muhammad by the angel Gabriel.

'Gabriel revealed one just like it to me!' he announced and proceeded to recite,

'The elephant, who told you about the elephant? It has a tail like a rope and a very long nose. It is one of God's creatures' (*sic!*).

He also produced a fake version of the chapter entitled, 'al-Kawthar' that went:

'We have given you jewels, so choose what you will. But be quick about it and do not be greedy!' He distorted other chapters in a similarly facile way.

Some of Musaylima's tribe had seen or heard that when Muhammad placed his hand on the head of a bald man, the hair grew back, or if he spat in a dried-up well, it filled with fresh water. If he spat in the eye of a blind man or of someone suffering from ophthalmia, the sight would be restored, while if he placed his hand on a child's head and said, 'May he live for one hundred years!' the child would live to be a hundred.

'Have you seen what Muhammad can do?' they asked him.

'I can do better than that,' was Musaylima's reply.

But in trying to imitate the Prophet, this enemy of God would place his hand on the head of a balding man and what little hair he had fell out. If he spat in a well, the water either dried up or turned salty, and by spitting in the eye of someone suffering from ophthalmia, he became permanently blind there and then. When he laid his hand on a child's head and said, 'Live for a hundred years!' the child immediately dropped down dead.

Just look, my friends, at what the scoundrel got up to! Success is in God's hands alone to grant or to withhold.

Now, in those days, there was a woman by the name of Sajah, from the tribe of Banu Tamim, who also claimed prophecy. Both she and Musaylima had heard of each other. Once, some time after the death of the Prophet Muhammad, she announced to a full war party of her tribe,

'Prophets do not come in pairs. Either he is a prophet and we shall all follow him or I am one and he and his tribe shall follow me.'

So she sent him a message, of which the content was:

'Prophecy does not coincide in two people at one time. Let us meet among a gathering of our two tribes and together examine what we have received in the way of revelation. Whoever speaks the truth shall be the one to follow.'

She sealed it and told the messenger,

'Take this letter to the Yamama and give it to Musaylima ibn Qays. I will follow later with the army.'

The next day, she and her tribe broke camp.

When he opened the letter and read its contents, Musaylima grew alarmed. He asked each member of his tribe for advice on what to do but no one could give him a satisfactory answer. He was in a state of some anxiety when an old man came up to him.

'Calm down, Musaylima, relax! I'm going to give you a little fatherly advice.'

'Let's have it, then. I need all the advice I can get.'

'Tomorrow morning, pitch a vaulted tent of coloured brocade just outside the camp. Spread silks and sprinkle perfumed waters – lily, rose, carnation, violet and the like. Fill censers with Khymer aloes, ambergris and musk, and perfume the interior. Loosen the tent ropes so none of the incense escapes and once the damp canvas has absorbed the smoke, take your seat and send for her. Invite her to join you alone in the tent. Once inside, the scent of the incense and perfume will relax and unwind her and she'll begin to lose control. At that point, take advantage of her and she will do whatever you want. Screw her and rid yourself of the wickedness of her and her tribe.'

'Well spoken,' said a reassured Musaylima. 'That's the best advice I've had.'

He did exactly as the old man had suggested and when Sajah arrived, invited her into the tent for private discussions. Sure enough, as they talked, she became steadily more and more confused. Aware that her distraction was sexual, he recited this poem to her:

> *The bedroom's prepared, pray let us go through,*
> *Lie down on your back, I'll show something to you,*
> *Take it bending or squatting, on your hands and*
>   *your knees,*
> *Take two-thirds or all of it, whatever would please!*

'All of it! Yes, all of it!' she cried. 'Show me everything, you prophet!'

So he jumped on top of her and had his way.

'When I've gone, ask my people for my hand in marriage,' she said afterwards.

She left him later and returned to her tribe.

'What do you think?' they asked.

'Well, he revealed his prophethood to me and I found him upright and upstanding, so I submitted to him!'

Her people consented to give her to Musaylima in marriage and in response to their demand for a dowry, he told them they need not observe the afternoon prayer. To this day, the tribe of Tamim do not observe that prayer, claiming that, as the dowry of their prophetess, it is their exclusive right. She was the only woman ever to have claimed prophecy and about her, one of the poets of Tamim composed these lines:

> *Our prophet was a woman, around her we trod,*
> *While men one and all were the prophets of God.*

Musaylima was eventually killed during the reign of the first Caliph, Abu Bakr Siddiq. Opinions differ as to who killed him. Some say it was Zayd ibn al-Khattab, while others claim it was Wahshi, another of the Prophet's Companions. I believe it was Wahshi, on the basis of his statement that he 'killed the best of men in the time of ignorance before Islam, Hamza ibn Abdalmuttalib, and the worst after the coming of Islam, Musaylima. May God forgive me for the former by virtue of the latter.' As for Sajah, she saw the error of her ways and repented, accepting Islam and marrying one of the Prophet's companions.

II

> *This contest of wits over a piece of brocade humorously symbolizes the gender battle. Also, here's a raunchy example of that female lust and resourcefulness we hear about in medieval Arab tales.*

During the reign of the Caliph Ma'moun, there lived a character by the name of Bahloul who was something of a jester and a frequent butt of jokes by the royal family and courtiers. One day, so the story goes, no sooner had he entered the court and been invited to sit down than the Caliph slapped him across the back of the head.

'What brings you here, you son of a whore?' He laughed.

'I've come to see my master, may God send him victorious,' replied Bahloul.

'How are you getting on with your two women?' asked the Caliph, aware that Bahloul had recently taken a second wife.

'Sire, I'm powerless to control the new one, the old one's a law unto herself and I'm staring poverty in the face.'

'If you can put that into verse, Bahloul, we're listening,' said the Caliph.

So Bahloul recited,

> *Poverty holds me in its chains, it tortures and torments,*
> *God has forsaken such as me and mankind shows*
> *contempt.*
> *If my poverty continues, without change to my position,*
> *Then I will be, quite certainly, homeless and in perdition.*

'And where would you go?' asked the Caliph.

'To God, His Messenger, and to you, Commander of the Faithful.'

'Well said! Whoever seeks refuge in God and His Messenger – and us – we welcome. Now, have you perhaps given expression to your marital predicament in verse, too, Bahloul?'

'I have indeed, Sire.'

'Come on, then, let's hear it!'
So Bahloul recited this poem:

> *I've taken two wives, poor fool that I am,*
> *I thought I'd be pampered in bed like a lamb,*
> *Lying in clover 'twixt two pairs of breasts*
> *But instead I find nightly I'm put to the test*
> *By two ravenous wolves who take nights in turn*
> *And in giving one pleasure, the other's rage burns.*
>
> *Each night there is constant abuse and derision,*
> *One woman's enough for two whole divisions!*
> *So take my advice for an honourable life*
> *And live as a bachelor, without trouble and strife*
> *But if that is something that cannot be done*
> *Then from that awful regiment, take only one!*

This sent the Caliph into a fit of laughter and he rewarded Bahloul with the gift of a very fine golden tunic. And so, in much better spirits than when he had arrived, Bahloul made his exit.

On his way home, he passed by the residence of the Grand Vizier where Hamdouna, the Caliph's sister and wife of the Vizier, was at home in her observatory. She happened to look down and see him.

'There's Bahloul, and wearing a golden tunic,' she remarked to her maid. 'Now, how can I take that off him?'

'You won't be able to, Madam.'

'I can outsmart that one.'

'Bahloul's a shrewd man, Madam. People think they're laughing at him but really he's the one who's laughing. Leave him alone or he'll drop you in the pit that you would dig for him.'

'I want that tunic!' Hamdouna insisted, and sent the maid to fetch him.

'My mistress invites you inside,' she said.

'One should always accept an invitation,' Bahloul replied, and followed her into the palace.

'I think you've come to listen to my singing, haven't you, Bahloul?' Hamdouna said. In fact, she was a very fine singer.

'That's right, Madam.'

'And afterwards, you'd like a little refreshment, would you not?'

'I would indeed, Madam,' he agreed.

So she sang to him in a quite lovely voice and afterwards had food and drink brought. Then she continued,

'Bahloul, I do believe you'd like to take off that fine tunic you have on and give it to me, wouldn't you?'

'There is one condition, Madam. I made a promise to myself I'd only give it to the woman who lets me do with her what a man does with his wife.'

'And what would you know about that, Bahloul?'

'Ha! God gave me all the talents to please! I know all there is to know about the needs and wants of women. There's no man more skilful than me!'

Now, Hamdouna was a very beautiful woman, the most attractive of her day. Otherwise brave men who saw her were humbled and lowered their gaze for fear of her God-given, siren-like charms. Any man who dared look into her eyes was bewitched and many were the heroes she had ruined. She had, in the past, sent notes to Bahloul but he had always turned her down, afraid that he, too, would end up bewitched by this *femme fatale*. And there the matter had remained – until that day, that is.

They settled into conversation. Sometimes he looks straight at her and sometimes his eyes do not leave the ground. Whenever she tries to tempt him into parting with the tunic, he teases her by talk of how much it will cost.

'Which is?' she wants to know.

'Intimacy, Madam!' he replies.

'And what would you know about that?'

'The lot! Women are my speciality. No one takes the care that I do on the job. In affairs of this world, Madam, men's motives and desires are very different. Some men give and some men take, some men buy and some men sell. Not me. All that interests me is making love, attending to the needs of pussies in distress and satisfying women's thirst.'

This kind of talk rather appealed to her.

'If you've written any verses about that, Bahloul, I would like to hear them,' says she.

So Bahloul recites:

Mankind may differ in wealth and in fame,
In conduct and custom and deeds they have done,
Some enjoy good name while others know shame,
There are some who have fortune and those who have none.

But I care not for things by which others are led,
Be they Arab or Turkish or Persian –
Only women in bed, whether virgin or wed
And the wonderful act of coition!

To your honour and rank I accord the respect
Of a slave, humble in front of his mistress
But I did not expect that you would reject
My proposal of passionate congress.

As a lover, no woman has known me to tire,
Of that you may have heard mention,
Is it not your desire that I cool down your fire
With this member of splendid dimension?

You will marvel indeed at its vigour and lust,
To self-doubt, it pays no attention;
By quenching your thirst, when I mount you and thrust,
You will know it has just one intention.

Now let me caress you, reject me no more,
Don't deny he who loves you your love,
If once only should bore you, why then I implore you
To fuck me 'til you've had enough!

So lie down beside me, attend to my prick,
It suffers the pain of rejection.
I play you no trick, for it is truly sick –
Be a nursemaid and treat my erection!

And there's no need to fear for your virtuous name,
Of what people would say if they knew.
You will not be blamed, disgraced, scorned or shamed,
Since no one will know but we two!

Listening to this, Hamdouna begins to relax and can't stop herself glancing at Bahloul's erection, straight as a flagpole, in front of her. She doesn't know what to do but soon the lust rising warm between her legs takes control. The Devil makes her blood hot and the thought of bedding him excites her.

'If he does it to me and shouts his mouth off afterwards, no one will ever believe him,' she reasons.

'Take off the tunic and come up to my bedroom, Bahloul.'

'It's yours once I get what I want!'

Aching and shaking with lust for him, she rises and makes her way upstairs, undoing her belt as she goes.

'Am I dreaming,' wonders Bahloul, as he follows, 'or is this for real?'

Entering the bedroom, she lies down upon the silk sheets of her bed. With her skirt above her thighs and her God-given loveliness on full display, she begins to caress herself in front of him. He gazes at her belly's gentle swell and the broadness of her navel, drawing breath upon her naked thighs and the marvellous thing between them, fluttering like a flag in a gentle breeze. He goes down on her and kisses her repeatedly. She slips into a swoon and starts to stroke him up and down, hardly aware of what she's doing.

'Madam, what a state you're in!'

'You son of a bitch!' she moans. 'I was like a mare on heat before and now you've made it quite unbearable. Your kind of talk could undo a saint. Your words are lethal!'

'But you're a married woman, so how come you're so hot?'

'What has married got to do with it? Some women get turned on by talk and others, if they've not done it for a while, can get turned on by any man – like a mare does by a stallion. Talk turns me on *and* I've not been speaking to my husband. So get on with it because he usually comes home about now!'

'My back hurts and I can't mount you. Why don't you get on top and do it? Then you can have the tunic and let me be on my way.'

Bahloul lies down on his back, as a woman would do for a man, his penis upright like a flagpole. Hamdouna sits astride him and takes hold of it. She admires it, amazed – and delighted – by its splendid size.

'This is a woman's ruin,' she gasps. 'I've *never* seen one as big as yours, Bahloul!'

She holds him against herself, easing it into her then slides down onto him and the whole thing vanishes inside her.

'God damn women!' laughs Bahloul. 'They're always losing things!'

She starts bouncing up and down, stirring it around and squeezing him inside her, until the two of them climax together. She takes hold of it again and eases herself off him, slowly.

'This is a man!' She sighs, gazing at it.

She wipes it for him then he gets up and makes to leave.

'And where's the tunic?'

'Madam, you've just fucked me. What more do you want?'

'You told me your back hurt and that you couldn't do it.'

'I never thought you'd do it to me. Now you owe me one and it will be my turn to do it. That's what the tunic costs and then you can discharge me.'

Well, I've come this far, she thinks, as she cuddles up to him again. He'll go once we've done it a second time.

'I'll only do it if you undress completely,' he tells her.

Hamdouna takes off all her clothes and Bahloul can only marvel at the beauty of her fully naked body. From top to bottom, he explores every part of her, before again arriving at that place.

'Ah! This is a man's enslavement,' he whispers, as he licks and kisses it over and over until her climax comes close.

She takes hold of him, guides him inside her and they begin to rock and roll until, eventually, they come.

'Off with the tunic!' she shouts, as he's about to leave.

'But that's us all square now.'

'Are you making fun of me?'

'The tunic is yours when you've paid for it,' he insists.

'How much?' she demands, glaring at him.

'You had the first one and I got the second, so that makes us equal. A third time and it's paid for,' he tells her, taking off the tunic, folding it and placing it in front of her.

'Do what you want!' she sighs, opening her legs once more.

He mounts her and slips it inside while she, pushing hard against him, matches all his movements until they come together. Then he gets up and goes, leaving the tunic behind him.

'Didn't I tell you that Bahloul's a sharp character,' said the maid, 'and that you wouldn't get the better of him? But did you believe me?'

'Shut up!' snapped Hamdouna. 'What happened, happened. Every pussy has its lover's name upon it, for better or for worse. If mine had not had Bahloul's on it, he would not have had me with a present of the world and everything within it.'

Suddenly there was a knock upon the door.

'Who's there?' asked the maid.

'Bahloul,' came the reply.

The Vizier's wife was surprised to hear his voice.

'What do you want?' asked the maid.

'A drink of water!'

The maid took him out a jug of water but after he had drunk, Bahloul let the jug drop on the ground and smash. The maid slammed the door and left him sitting there. Presently, the Vizier came home.

'What are you doing here, Bahloul?'

'Sir, I was passing and got taken thirsty so I knocked on the door and the maid brought me a jug of water but it slipped from my hands and broke and, by way of compensation, Madam Hamdouna took the tunic that our master, the Commander of the Faithful, had given me.'

'Bring the tunic here!' ordered the Vizier.

Hamdouna appeared at the door.

'Did you make Bahloul pay for a broken jug with that priceless tunic?'

'Is that how it was, Bahloul?' she asked, clasping her hands.

'I've explained what happened in my artless way, Madam, now you tell it with finesse!'

Speechless, she handed him the tunic, which he slipped on and went upon his way.

Powder Figures

I love Ananda Devi's vibrant resurrection of this Indian myth, her perceptive look at the different relationships of two women to their own bodies and the complex interplay of the sexual and the spiritual.

They lit the room with carmine lamps and sent men to remote parts of the forest to look for the most fragrant blossoms, the night *kali*, the flower of love, that would drown all other smells in its unbearable sweetness. With this flower, they garlanded all the columns and arches, and they drew on the floor propitious shapes in many-coloured powders, meant to awaken and sustain desire even in the most desireless one. Some went as far as telling the story that had not yet taken place: drawn by the power of the mantras that had been recited in this very room only moments before, they let their imagination run wild and, from their nimble fingers, used to producing abstract and geometric shapes on the marble floors for the many festivals of the lunar calendar, emerged soft womanly curves, unclothed except for the colouring of love, as well as dark and ungainly, yet curiously attractive, manly shapes. These they coupled in a thousand ways, hoping against hope that the woman who would enter

the room in a short while would read the drawings and surrender to their potency. Musicians they placed in the
adjoining room, telling them to play the sweetest and most
suggestive music they had ever played, the vagrant tunes
meant to spur on kings when they thought themselves spent
among their concubines and yet wanted to go on because the
remaining ones were as lovely as, if not lovelier than, the
ones who had already pleasured and been pleasured and
their skin was now glowing dark with the effort of their
waiting, and their lips had become red from the bite of their
impatience, and their light silk garments were showing dark
patches where their desire had seeped through, and their
smell was enough to drive the king mad even if his noble
organ was now limp and sore. And so this music, meant to
revive the king during his nightly pleasures so that dawn
would find him drowned in a swelter of flesh and moistness
and swollen lips and mustardy and musty smells, incapable
of knowing where he began and ended and whose was the
breast throbbing in his mouth and whose the warm mounds
his hand was holding and whose the juicy mouth closed
about him, was now to find a new, strange and totally unnatural role: it was meant to awaken the desire of a queen.

They flitted in and out, anxious to follow the old queen's
instructions. It was against their own inclination: they felt for
the young queens, especially for the first. She would be the
first to face the unknown. They had seen her face as she
heard the decision. They had read the utter horror in her
eyes, the beginning of a refusal on her mouth, her hand,
rising as if to stay the words before they were uttered. But
then reason and duty asserted themselves once again. The

old queen had spoken, there was no possible refusal. Everything was sealed with a nod of her head, and she was the one who told her younger sister. The two women were again locked in their symmetrical fate. They sat and talked and sighed. The elder one cried, the younger one rebelled, but silently, as always. As they had done when Bhishma, the prince, had swept them away from their father's home and claimed them as brides. They had loved him then, loved his beauty, his courage, his warrior-like demeanour and wise countenance, and the marks of greatness glowing on his forehead that singled him out from among all the kings seeking their hand. But then, after carrying them away, he had revealed the bitter truth: he had chosen them not for himself but for his brother, the king, because *he* had made a vow of celibacy. He had done so to allow his father to marry a fisherman's daughter, the beautiful Satyavati of the thousand fragrances, because that was the condition she had set. She was to be queen and her children were to inherit the kingdom, so he, Bhishma, the king's firstborn, had taken that terrible vow of chastity until the gods quailed and showered flowers upon him in admiration.

The two sisters had cried and pleaded, but they had no say in the matter. Such things were decided and decreed long before, as part of a long chain of causes and effects and purposes and results, and the gods and kings held the supreme power to decide and decree. No such choice fell upon them.

And so they were brought to Bhishma's brother, the king, as his wives, and had to live with the one whom they always thought of, secretly wrinkling their fastidious noses, as the fisherwoman's son. They could never love him, yet did their duty as his queens. Except that they bore no children. They did their best. Drank everything that could be drunk, ate everything that could be eaten, fasted on alternate days until they turned into shadows of their old selves, but to no avail. Again they lamented their fate, which had taken away the man who should have continued the noble line, except for his baseless vow never to marry and never to have children, and had given them a husband who could not even offer them the joy of motherhood.

Now the king was dead without a son, and the old queen had sat for days and nights thinking and ruminating about this, feeling that the end of so great a lineage was too heavy a responsibility to bear, that it would spoil her karma for ever and condemn her to an ignominious rebirth as a servant girl or as a slave or as a vulture gorging on corpses. She could not bear this, she who had risen from fisherman's daughter to king's wife! Then it was that the oddest plan came to her mind. She could not ask the queens to sleep with any man, even if he were to be a king. This would be a sin that would condemn her to an endless series of even lower rebirths. But it was acceptable for pure women to sleep with saintly men, as their seed was a blessing for the whole line. A *rishi* was both more and less than a man: more spirit than flesh, he could not be accused of lusting for the queens. He would come and do his duty and leave them gloriously pregnant without any shame falling on the sisters. And who better than the ancient Vyasa could do this for them? He was, after all, a half-brother to the king.

For a full second, the old queen visualized the *rishi* as she had last seen him, and shuddered. Taller than ordinary men, he was skeleton thin, only wearing an old piece of bark, his dark skin encrusted with earth, mud, dust, leaves, dung and other unnameable things. He left a trail of dirt wherever he went and smelt like a corpse long dead. His long matted hair crawled with living creatures. His toenails were horrendously twisted and made a grating sound as he walked. But this was nothing compared to his face. Vyasa's face was like no human face. His centuries of asceticism had transformed it into something neither human nor divine, but rather monster-like. A third eye looked as if it had been scraped open in the middle of his forehead. His nose had almost disappeared because of his meditation posture, lying face down for years on end. His lips were parched, shrivelled pieces of skin. His teeth had long fallen out, and his bare gums were black. His beard was entangled with his hair and covered his hollow chest. And his eyes burned. They were mostly closed, even when he came among the living. But if he happened to open them, you could see that they were red, and no longer saw the world as it was but as it had ever been, with layers upon layers of history and decay and falsehood, and deep down, the inner meaning that he alone knew and understood. You could not look into these eyes. Anyone who dared to do so would die out of sheer despair, unable to bear the emptiness that he would see in his own self. Everyone had the wisdom to bow in front of the saint and never to look up.

But what would the queens do? The old queen pondered this. She did not want them to die. She did not want them to show disrespect to the saint either. But would they be able to hide their repulsion and horror? Would they be able to survive their fear? She questioned their mettle. They were not like her. She had made things happen. They allowed things to happen. They had bent to Bhishma's will, to the king's will and now they would bend to her will. How would they nurture future kings? She was no longer sure. But this was no time for uncertainty. Something was pressing her to act. She asked her attendants to go and tell the queens about her decision. She did not want to see them squirm.

They were preparing the elder sister. She had submitted without protest, and had been brought to the bathing room where miraculous fragrances were rising from the milk bath. Full-blown roses were floating in it. In each, a tiny candle in a gemstone holder had been lit. The gems shone blue and red and green, creating wonderful patterns of translucent light on the surface. Songbirds were twittering in gold cages. The queen was made to walk over a bed of petals and, standing in front of a window opening out on to the night sky, the humming spring breeze drifting in and out, she allowed them to undress her. They removed the silk veils that hid her hair and covered her bodice. Then they untied the laces of the bodice itself, freeing her full white breasts with the nipples echoing the dark hue of the roses. The freshness of the breeze made them harden, and the attendant girls giggled, then went suddenly quiet when they remembered what was waiting for the queen. They yearned to console her, to cover her with their own bodies, to protect her from the pending ordeal. But they were not allowed to show any compassion. They were to pretend that this was like any nuptial night where the queen would meet the king and was to be made beautiful for him. And she was, so very beautiful, standing naked now except for the exquisite jewellery that she never removed, hanging between her breasts, over her rounded belly, about her waist and arms and wrists and ankles – chains, perhaps, that tied her to her fate.

They undid the clasps from her hair and let it fall blackly to her buttocks. It moved against her back, making her feel suddenly languid. The incense burning in a corner was heady. She thought that they must have put some special powder in it to make her dizzy and light-headed. She stepped into the bath as the girls moved the candles away from her. The warm scent rushed to her head, and she sat down heavily, lay against the curved marble surface and put her head back on to the cushions ready for her. She looked at her hair, floating in long lazy tentacles about her, and extended her arms and legs as the girls began to rub her body with an oily paste. They took their time, kneading her shoulders, arms, breasts, all her body, even between her legs and buttocks, letting her feel their teasing fingers until she was completely aroused, but not allowing her pleasure to peak. When they reached her toes she was almost unbearably ready, but they stopped as if on cue, made her stand up, loose-limbed and breathless, and washed her with warm jasmine-scented water. They dried her, rubbed another lighter paste to make her body shine and smell like a wildly blossoming garden, brushed her hair long and lovingly, but left it loose, and wound about her silk robes so delicately woven that they were almost transparent, and covered her body with nothing but a golden sheen.

Then, thus prepared, they brought her to the room where they had earlier carried out their magic and made her lie down on a bed so soft that it was whispering against her back while the silk rubbing against her skin was whispering to the front of her body. They left her when the music started. Her body was ready, but her mind was aghast.

Show him no disrespect. Receive him as you would the most beautiful of princes, or gods.

She had tried to convince herself that it was an honour. But now, as she waited, the fullness of her desire ebbing swiftly, her eyes wandering, sightless, on the drawings that, had she seen them would only have seemed to taunt her, it was fear that filled her mind. Fear of looking at him and dying. Fear of not looking at him but smelling, hearing and feeling him. Fear of angering him. Fear of arousing him. Fear of not arousing him. Fear of running away. Fear of fear.

She heard noises. Steps. A door opening. A door closing. She breathed slowly and recited a mantra to calm herself. She closed her eyes. Now that the moment had come, she knew what she had to do. She had to see it through, not because of the queen's order, not because of the king's impotence, not because of her duty, but because she wanted to have a son who would live to become a great king and carve his and her own name in destiny's flesh. She would not submit to fate but be part of it, help shape it and give it her secret mark, immerse herself into the timeless web of things and people and events that had made the world what it was, so that without her tiny being, the whole gigantic structure would fall apart.

He had stopped in front of the bed and was looking at her, she knew. She knew that, in some faraway place, she was lying on the bed and was shaking with revulsion at the thought of this creature – almost an animal – standing close to her, smelling of rot and decay, crawling with maggots and

lice, touching her, pawing her, opening her with his claw-like
nails, mixing with her, penetrating her, polluting her with his
dirt and slime and odour of death. Somewhere, she did not
know where, a queen was heaving with the disgust of this
offering and this sacrifice to some higher order and purpose
that she had never understood.

But in this place, in this now, in this here, her eyes were
still closed, and his presence was so immense that it was as if
she was looking at him and, indeed, seeing him as he really
was, a burning shape without flesh, just a soul, a blinding
soul not full of goodness, because he was beyond that, but
full of – of what? She could not name it. Full of being, she
then thought. The room was whirling about her. She smelt
nothing, saw none of the horrific sights that usually met
those who dared look upon Vyasa. She was bathed in light
and warmth. Once again, she felt she was ready.

Something, not touching her at all, moved the gossamer
fabric that covered her, away from her breasts, away from
her belly, away from her thighs. She heard it sizzle and burn
briefly, and she grew even more afraid of his touch. But still
she did not move. She allowed his eyes to travel over her
naked body, as if drinking her in. She began to feel both hot
and cold, her nipples rose as she waited, beads of sweat
sparkled over her body and her juices began to flow. But still
he did not touch her. Then she remembered. He had never
slept in a bed.

Still blind, she got up from the bed, and lay down on the
marble floor, arms raised above her head, legs apart, offering
herself entirely.

He was looking still, a creature beyond age who had
almost forgotten the shape of woman. He was silent and

surprised. He who had thought this a perfunctory act, a disdainful gift to the small wishes of people who called themselves kings but were only pawns in the hands of the gods, knowing full well where all this would lead to and how brief these lives were going to be, hardly a spark in the earth's soft and strong belly, he was now taken aback by the power that lay in the body beneath him, and in the promises that it was offering him. He saw her, too, as she was. A young woman afraid, and yet capable of going beyond fear to touch upon some eternal truths. This strength, in so young, so childlike a being, filled him with wonder. He also saw the possibilities in awakening such a thing to true knowledge. He knew now why the gods needed this coupling that he despised, this other, whom he thought futile, to be complete: they were two halves that needed to come together in this brief, yet perfect moment.

His breath licked her, all of her: her eyes, her lips, her tongue, her armpits, her breasts, her belly, her pubis, her vulva, her thighs, her feet. His fingers, without touching, played with all the places that he had forgotten about and saw them tremble with this awakening. His nostrils breathed in her smells. His tongue tasted her tears, sweat, and the salty-sweet liquid between her legs. His ears heard her low song, her groans rising to high-pitched birdlike cries. A deep longing was rising in him. A violent need to be with her and in her, not as a god, finally, but simply as a man whom she could love. He was being pulled towards her, fully erect, his head was spinning, he could not wait any longer. He knelt and urged her legs even more open, looking at the immeasurably soft, glistening folds waiting for him.

She felt him kneel down, and then sensed, in one sharp moment, an intense heat, an incredible surge of painful power between her legs, almost as if she had been lifted and impaled. She nearly shouted, but she bit her lips and swallowed back her tears, letting the burning burrow inside her, deep, deep inside where it would meet with that part of her that was ready to receive and to generate. She allowed the heat to spread out inside her belly. She felt herself joined to him in an enormous joy. *Become a son, become a king, become a god*, she thought.

But as the burning went on and on, she saw a hundred sons come out of this single son of hers, and they began to run all over her body as if it were a battlefield, and they began to kill others who were like brothers, and to kill themselves until what was left was ashes. Her progeny would come to naught.

She heard him then, though he was silent. 'You are right, your progeny will come to naught. But it is needed to teach a great lesson to mankind.'

Then, as an afterthought, the voice added: 'You gave me pleasure, but you closed your eyes. Because of this, your son will be born blind.'

Underneath her, the powder figures that had been frantically coupling all night were smudged and destroyed.

The queen lay there with the sad smile of knowledge and acceptance.

Her sister would make no such mistake.

She, too, had been prepared, on the following night, but the intricate rituals of preparation did not move her or arouse her. Her body was taut and trembling with energy

and fury. She would show no fear, no weakening, no graceful giving. She would take from him and not give in to the
elaborate lies of lovemaking. She was dark and lovely as a
clouded moon. She shone, but inwardly; her body was lithe
and serpent-like. Her eyes neither faltered nor flattered. Her
pride clothed her more than the red garments they had
wound about her body, the *dhoti* that snaked about her thighs
and buttocks and belly and would need to be carefully
unwrapped or roughly torn away, the veil that covered her
breasts but did not hide their glorious swell and purple, hard
tips, the thin gold laces they had tied about her fleshy arms
and her waist and that symbolized, for her, only the bondage
of womanhood.

They had redrawn the figures on the floor. Had mixed
with the powders strange essences only known to them, to
give them even more potency. They were no longer sure of
what they were doing. These rituals were not customary,
but they could not bear to see the cowering remnants of the
figures they had drawn earlier torn apart by the saint and
by his final curse, so perfunctorily uttered, as if having a
blind son would not tear the queen apart too, and leave her
regretting every single slow second of what remained of
her tragic life, that single act of cowardice. They wanted
these drawings to replace the flawed shapes and anguished
faces of real life. They wanted this coupling to be more perfect than it could ever be in truth. They opened lips and hips
wide and drew the world inside the bellies of the female
shapes, and dotted the male bodies with signs of elevated
goodness and sainthood. But their fear of Vyasa still seeped
through and tainted these shapes with a mixture of cruelty
and wanton violence. The female figures, though exquisitely

and ecstatically drawn, had the pale hues of repulsion, however dark the colours they mixed with their agile fingers.

Now the young sister waited. She would not lie down but prowled about, unaware of how dangerously her body moved. Her hennaed feet, the patterns not quite dry, left dark smudges on the marble tiles, in the circular space remaining unadorned about the bed. She had never looked upon the saint, but had heard people describe him, and thought she knew what to expect. *A foul-smelling mendicant, crawling with bugs!* she thought, with a harsh laugh. *I will make it as short as possible, bear what has to be borne, take what is given and go.* She rubbed the sweet-smelling paste off her body, not wanting to attract him and encourage him to linger. She smudged the kohl that rimmed her eyes until she looked like a haunted animal with disc-like eyes. Then she thought it would be quicker if she were naked. She began to remove her clothes.

And so it was that he entered and surprised her in complete disarray – hair dishevelled, lips violent with anger, veil half pulled away, revealing a single, gorgeous breast, brown belly bare down to the tightly curled pubic hair that masked the red cleft beneath, *dhoti* half torn off, creating a chequered pattern of red and brown. She had one arm raised above her shoulder, one leg lifted to remove the *dhoti*, pushing back her buttocks into an even more voluptuous roundness – a pose so like the temple statues in their frenzy of love that the saint himself was arrested by this vision.

Still filled with the experience of the night before, he moved in one swift step towards her to join in her dance.

She, taken unawares and unprepared, could only look. Her brain took a long time to register what she was seeing:

a shape, dense, brittle, bristling with sharp angles, emerging from the candle-lit depths of the room; a noise like a thousand crabs mating, clicking, crackling; a smell like a pit-hole full of dankness and noisome substances and growths; a sensation of utter horror and despair, that made her hair fan out of its own accord, that made goose-pimples rise over her entire body, and her mouth open into a perfect circle of fear. The unnameable thing was moving towards her, and there was nothing she could do. Looking down, she saw the lovely shapes the women had drawn for her – for them. The endless coupling, all the possible positions that a man and a woman could take to touch each other well and truly, in all the places that could be touched and tasted. The openness of the woman, unlocked in this instant of eternity, and the sharp pointedness of the man, ready to slide in, to penetrate, to release, to regenerate. She saw the abandon of the women, singing out loud their pleasure. The gauntness of the men, spent, and yet filled with the sap of this relentless, ageless energy. Lies, an infinite string of lies, all the more sorrowful because they were so beautiful.

He was very near now. She, frozen in this standing position, incapable of moving back, even as the thick, crawling shadows that surrounded him engulfed her too. His face, as it reached hers, caught a fragment of light broken off from a dying candle. Thus did she see it in this half-light, and it was enough; she paled, and her face turned a greyish hue, and her skin became parchment-like, and her hair went white, as if, in a fraction of a second, she had aged and lost all pretence of youth.

He, amused in some remote way by her horror and the refusal beneath, merely extended a hand and took hold of one end of her veils, like a silky skein of blood between his fingers, and began to unwind them. His will soared to subdue hers. And, like a puppeteer holding a live being at the end of his strings, he made her dance. Moved her in graceful cadences, slow and immeasurably sensual. Arms raised and sinuously beckoning, waist swaying, breasts murmuring, belly undulating, legs throbbing with their own dense rhythms, feet drumming, she danced in the tightness of her fear, hearing echoes of laughter and music from the gods, locked in the terrible eyes that ripped her open to look upon the core of fragility and utter weakness and malleability that had lain hidden for years, even from herself.

Round and round about the room she went, her veils now entirely gone, revealing a body at once proud of its beauty and shamed by its own nakedness. And as she danced, she drew and entrained with her the female shapes on the floor, so that the whole room rippled with their silent twirling, the misty colours swirling about her with their ever-changing patterns of dark and light.

She lost count of time. She did not know at what moment he joined her and began to dance with her. And what irresistible melody he hummed into her ear, chuckling like a running brook and whispering with the air. She only knew that there was grace and beauty and joy, and a longing that she had never felt before, so that the restless, angry energy that had filled her for so long with a bitter draught turned into the raw, iron-hot urge of desire.

It was like a strange, incongruous re-enactment of the *Ras Lila*, love-dance of Krishna and of his love-swept *gopis*, but in which the players, both human and of coloured powder, knew their role and their purpose, and also the simple fact that they did not exist at all.

They ran through the gamut of playful joinings. He could move in unimaginable ways, he was everywhere, over her and inside her, and her supple body matched his in opening out to be reached and to reach, lips and hips wide apart, a world of love in her belly. And thus the coupling took place, in the middle of this wild dance, and the queen surrendered readily, and at long last, at the end of the night, came with a laugh. When they parted, she looked again at him, and smiled. He hesitated, caught unawares by this sweetness. Something tugged at him. He wanted to stay longer, just to hear her magnificent, triumphal, orgasmic laughter again. As he looked at her sated flesh, soft with dewy moistness and purpled by his caresses, her loose-limbed contentment, a feeling stirred in some unknown place of his body. His heart, probably, which had long been asleep as he conquered, one by one, every human failing, except those of pride and indifference.

But it had been asleep far too long. And the paleness of her face, the visible signs of her initial horror, again became apparent to him, and the age-old habits of power settled once more heavily about his shoulders.

Without even thinking about it, he uttered, voicelessly: 'You are exquisitely beautiful, but you turned pale from revulsion when you saw me. Because of this, your son will be born an albino.'

And he left.

The queen looked at the door with uncomprehending eyes. And as she did so, all the tiny female shapes on the floor turned and did the same.

The queen who would give birth to Pandu the Pale, father of the Pandavas, and would thus witness the destruction of the entire race of the Kurus from sheer fratricidal rage, stood up and allowed the converging anger of all the three worlds to wash over her and drive away all memory of this night.

Sappho

This legendary poet creates a female love chain when she tries to ensure that her earthly love is requited, through the agency of her divine Beloved, Aphrodite, goddess of love. Body and spirit come together.

On the throne of many hues, Immortal Aphrodite,
child of Zeus, weaving wiles – I beg you
not to subdue my spirit, Queen,
with pain or sorrow

but come – if ever before
having heard my voice from far away
you listened, and leaving your father's
golden home you came

in your chariot yoked with swift, lovely
sparrows bringing you over the dark earth
thick-feathered wings swirling down
from the sky through mid-air

arriving quickly – you, Blessed One,
with a smile on your unageing face

asking again what have I suffered
and why am I calling again

and in my wild heart what did I most wish
to happen to me: 'Again whom must I persuade
back into the harness of your love?
Sappho, who wrongs you?

For if she flees, soon she'll pursue,
she doesn't accept gifts, but she'll give,
if not now loving, soon she'll love
even against her will.'

Come to me now again, release me from
this pain, everything my spirit longs
to have fulfilled, fulfil, and you
be my ally.

The Sacrifice

The annual marriage of the Goddess and sacrifice of the groom was an elaborate and painful ritual replicating the cutting of the harvest and the fertilization of the fields. The inevitable sense of grief symbolizes the incompatibility of a lasting union between mortal and god.

There she sat, in all her glory, the ancient bride, awaiting her young bridegroom. People scurried around her, handmaidens, attending her every whim, priests and priestesses making offerings, worshippers prostrating themselves, kissing her feet. But Attargatis knew their thoughts were not on the glories of the bride. They were all thinking of the sacrifice that was to follow.

Oh, not the chickens and the fish and the offerings of corn and wheat. Look at the bridegroom, Mithras, slowly being prepared in his chamber: spring incarnate, hardly touched by the first bloom of youth, his body lithe, lissom, luminous, covered in fine golden hairs like the flaxen strands that enfold the corn kernel. Golden and, like the sun, glowing. All eyes would be on him when he came out of his chamber, and rode through the streets on his sun-chariot, bathed in light, the ultimate offering – youth – on the altar of the ageless, infinite Attargatis.

It was the dazzling replay of life and death, the great cosmic tableau of continuity. Life conceived, life sacrificed: a display of the goddess in her infinite magnificence and munificence, expanding, filling up first with the life to come, then bursting forth, spilling her multiple bounties for the world to enjoy and celebrate. When the fields were high with waving sheaves of grain and the farmer and his family danced their dance of success and plenty, it was she, Attargatis, to whom they sang praise and gave thanks as they went into the fields in their scores, scythes in hand, filling their baskets with the crop. Never did they stop to question the process of reproduction: the planting of the seed in the Earth-womb, the conception of the crop, its growth to the height of its glory – its sacrifice at the peak of its perfection. For they knew well that once perfection had been reached, decay would shortly follow. So the harvest must be reaped, the corn must be milled, then eaten, to nourish, bring new life, new joy to all. And not one farmer forgot to set aside the most perfect of the grain to be returned to the Earth for absorption and regeneration.

And so it was with Attargatis and her son Mithras. She was the womb that conceived his life. She was the tomb that contained and warmed him in his death. She was the vessel that re-created and reproduced. It was no different from the corn, the wheat, or any other grain. Each year she, the Mother, revelled in the harvest. Pride and pleasure filled her heart as she watched the culmination. For the pinnacle of that great annual game of conception and destruction was the Sacred Marriage: her marriage to Mithras, the paramount jewel of her creation, the perfect being – the Sun. Her beloved son. Mithras, the golden child, the Child of the

Grain. The Master of Life on Earth. The life of her body. Attargatis knew how to keep him young, ever-living. He was the One who was eternally youthful, eternally in the bloom of growth and perfection. Beyond the moment of perfection lay decay – and he would never know the indignity of weakness, infirmity, old age. The sacrifice was all.

Her high priests and high priestesses prepared the rituals and ceremonies, said the prayers, prepared young Mithras for weeks beforehand, beautifying him, strengthening him, purifying him in preparation for the blessed moment. And with every action they praised Attargatis, begged for her blessings, appeased her so that she would be happy on the vital night of her marriage to Mithras. The night she would conceive, and ensure the continuation of the world for another year.

Strange to think that foreigners and outsiders were sometimes sceptical about the annual marriage of Attargatis to her son. They called her the Terrible Female. Goddess she might be but she was ancient and terrifying – and who knows, they thought, quaking, what she is like when she is alone in her chamber? Is she a foul hag, etched all over with wrinkles? Is her flesh putrid? And the orbs of her eyes, are they covered with a film that tinges them the green of phlegm? Is she in truth the same incandescent mountain of glory that they all see, or a shrivelled, pathetic bundle of lust and evil?

The thought was too hideous to hold long in the mind: an ugly old crone lusting after youth. Why, she might be no better than the monsters who waited each year for a virgin to be sacrificed. Yet her power was such that she succeeded in making people rejoice with her. Yes, yes, they knew that the annual death of Mithras ensured eternal life for him. That he was the grain child, the seed saved from the harvest and returned to the earth. But there was something obscene in that she bore him each year only to swallow him whole. This *hieros gamos*, this marriage game, this ritual without which the fields would not sprout, the sun would not shower down his bounty, it was beyond them. Wasn't Mithras the Sun incarnate, born from her womb and served to her at this ceremony? The marriage, perhaps, might better be called a funeral. After all, did it not end in the Feast of Blood?

The many who pondered these thoughts never allowed them to flicker from sparks into full-blown tongues of fire: they dreaded that if Attargatis knew what they were thinking, she might destroy them. Such was the summary justice of the goddess. Mother she may be, merciful she was not, if her order, her decree, was challenged. That was what they believed.

But in the enormity of her being, Attargatis knew their thoughts well. And she forgave them their lack of understanding. What mother holds the ignorance of her children against them? It was for her to reveal or conceal knowledge. She was the Earth, she was the Mother, the universal mother, responsible for peace, life and perpetuity. But her most important rite would always remain a mystery. For mortals would never understand the true meaning of eternity, that death was simply a station on the way. The ritual should have been all the explanation required. But from the thousands who attended each year only a handful, perhaps only the initiates, understood the true meaning of the death of Mithras, the Sun, as the secret of life's perpetuation. That he had to slough off his old body in order to be renewed. Did they not see the lesser sun in the winter, distant, nascent, growing? Did they not see how he became stronger, more powerful as the months progressed? Did that not tell them the importance of 'death', without which his old form would be exhausted, unable to contain his abiding energy?

Surely the truth was plain in the fields, which lay neatly in barren-looking rows of seeded soil, through the months of the lesser sun, growing silently concealed from sight until they began to sprout and growing to miraculous maturity. Nine months: the period of creation. What good were tender ears of wheat and corn if they were not severed from the well-spring at their peak? True, for a while the fields looked bleak and ruined after the cutting of the golden sheaves that had adorned them for the past weeks. But the old had always to make room for the new. Yet people found it impossible to separate themselves from the living present. They could not see that as far as the life cycle went, wheat, corn, humans were metaphors of each other.

No, Attargatis could not find it within herself to censure the uninitiated. Even she, great goddess, knower of all mysteries, was unable, when the moment came, to staunch her grief at the loss of her beloved. She didn't mourn the fields of corn and wheat. Yet when she, source of all being, was compelled to undergo the grief of her son's death, her lover's death, year after year, she too shed a tear. Though she knew that her marriage gift to Mithras, the sacrifice itself, was the gift of eternal life. Life in death, death in life. No one would ever know how deeply the knowledge of the all-knowing can wound the knower and with what pain the all-giving wrenches from his own being to give.

And now the moment was here: the moment for which she lived and in which she died each year. The moment in which her jubilation and perfection reached its height, and which she dreaded more than any other.

She sat on her throne, adorned in the colours of spring, summer and autumn, and smiled. All eyes were upon her. Attargatis was torn between mourning and rejoicing, between the transient immediacy of loss and the triumphal knowledge of eternal life. Perhaps it was as well that the rules of the Mysteries demanded that she contain her ambivalence. Or what would she have done? Bubbled with laughter and the thrill of anticipation, then lamented her loss?

And there came Mithras now, a blaze of glory, riding towards her on his white bull. A cheer went up. People shaded their eyes with their hands to see him better. All over Anatolia, effigies of Attargatis and Mithras were guided through the same rituals: she the bride, he the groom, brought forth to the people by the priests and priestesses, dressed in the garments of gods and goddesses, re-enacting the bloody drama upon their own bodies.

Here is Mithras, golden sun, spring-man, Attargatis' son and divine lover. He dismounts from his bull and walks to her, lithe-limbed, spare, gliding on winged feet. She fills with pride as she watches: he pauses to look at her, he approaches, walking along the processional route, scattering sunshine. She sees the stark desire on the faces of the women in the crowds, young and old. She feels a twinge, though she can't place the emotion behind it. Not envy, surely. She knows he has eyes only for her and the warmth of his gaze sends tremors of rapture through her. As if in answer to her thoughts, he smiles at her. They are truly one.

He is near her now, and stretches out his hand to take

hers. He brushes it with his lips as he kneels before her, head bowed.

Tenderly she detaches her hand, pausing a moment to stroke into place a curling golden tendril that has escaped from his crown to his forehead. Then, placing both palms against his temples, she raises him gently from the ground until her arms are high above her shoulders, garlanding his beloved face.

She sees only Mithras. For the first time she is apprehensive. But the ritual must proceed. She braces herself. The crowds are ready.

She addresses him with the words of the ritual. 'Welcome Mithras, my son-lover, soon to be the divine husband of the goddess. Let the ceremony begin.'

She sits down, emotion swelling inside her. 'The universal order above all,' she recites. 'I am here to serve the universe and its beings.' The words are as much a reminder to herself as part of the ceremony. Defiance, challenge – these are not for her. The cosmos must continue and it is fitting that she should pay the greatest price for it.

The chanting, the wedding-songs, the feasting, the fanfare and excitement wash over her as she is swept up in the joy of Mithras' encircling warmth. Each time they perform the sacred marriage, the oaths are fresh and new to her, the joy, the thrill of becoming his bride take hold of her, turn her into a mighty ocean of ecstasy splashing its spray and salt over all around. She whirls and leaps as she leads the crowds in a dance of celebration. Then, finally, she gives the command: 'Take to the fields in pairs. Lie together in the soil. Your actions will excite the earth until she opens herself up and becomes fertile. Your ecstasies will seep down into her.

Tonight the Earth will share in my divine marriage. Tonight she will conceive and, like me, take in and nurture the seed within her womb to pour forth at harvest.'

As the crowds took to the fields, laughing, singing, clinging to each other, lovers all, for a night, Attargatis led Mithras to her chamber. By her bed, she stood tremulous, nervous as any bride, in anticipation of love. Mithras approached her. She thought she saw a certain shyness in him. She stroked his cheek with her fingertips, running them featherlike over his soft golden beard.

She slid on to her couch and drew his head to her breast. His arms were around her waist, and his fingers caressed the ridge of her spine. His breath was soft and moist. He nuzzled against her, searching for her nipple. An image flashed before her of his baby face, his curls, his chubby infant hands groping for solace. Gently, urgently, she released her breasts and his warm lips closed around them in turn. With a moan she pressed his head to her. Mother-love vied with passion – her heart raged with both. Then the smooth, soft coming-together. Always one love melded into the other. Now it was the mother who took birth and life in the lover. She was the mother, she was the lover-consummate. To each other, they were all.

Mithras moved his head up her body, his hands were at her throat, grasping, stroking. She matched his ardour, curving her spine, straining to cover his shoulders in kisses. And now he was stretched over her, his feet tangling with hers as he entered her and they performed the sacred, celestial act of creation. At first, almost frantically, then slowly, as if time stood still. The vibration coursed through their bodies, a thunderous explosion as rain burst from his sky body into her earth form.

She felt his seed fill her womb, life passing from him to her.

Afterwards, he knelt before her as she stood, distraught. His head rested against her belly. She clung to it, holding him tight against her, and he raised his hands to hers.

'Why must I let you go again?' she murmured.

'Go?' he whispered, looking up at her with wide golden eyes. 'I have come home to my source. I'm not leaving you . . . I'll be closer inside you, with you, than at any other time.'

He caressed her flowing eyes, staying her sobs with a kiss that resonated deep within her ground.

'You glow in the dark,' he whispered.

Attargatis laughed. 'You say that every time.'

He laughed too. 'And so do you.'

'It's true,' they both said.

Attargatis stood up, walked to the window and looked out. There was a light in the chamber of the high priest. She flung together the curtains. Panic bleached her face so that her lips and eyes were etched against it dark and stark.

'Why?' she rasped. 'Why must it always be like this? Why must we be separated?'

Mithras smiled the wisdom of the world. 'This is not separation, my love. It is the closest, most unassailable union. In you, you surrounding me. We are indivisible. I breathe your breath, I eat your food. You grow with my growth. It is the way of things. The order. I am the Sun, you are the Moon. We cannot share the same sky for long. But we are creatures of the same light.'

Wise, so wise with the knowledge of endless centuries, yet so young, he holds out his arms and she enters them. An eternity passes, encapsulated in a single heartbeat. Then he stretches himself on the couch and folds his arms under his head. Attargatis lies down beside him, her head on his ribs. They hold each other close until she eases her curving body over him intent only on giving him pleasure. Now Mithras is the consummate lover. He holds her writhing hips gently between his palms, supporting her, encouraging her until they both reach the moment of complete union.

Outside there are sounds: the tambourine, the flute, the drums. They've never sounded so cruel, so ruthless. Mithras is her infant son again and she his weeping mother, arm supporting his head as she rocks him tenderly, cradling him against her bosom, singing soft comfort to him.

I'm the flower, she thinks, who never manages to fill her eye with the beauty of the bud. Grief-stricken because I've missed the warning of dawn's flower-bells. You lie asleep in the night-chambers of my passion, shaken awake by the transient melodies of love's breath. And once again this gust of music blows our way, bringing us tales of infinity.

The priests and priestesses enter, wreathed in smiles, bathed in music, clothed in ceremonies. Mithras goes with them.

Attargatis watches, proud, stately, dispassionate, as he leaves her to choose a spot beneath a tree in the shadow of his solar temple. As he approaches the sacred grove, he looks back once, a playful smile dancing in his eyes. She presses the palms of her hands to her belly. 'Your seed is inside me.'

Suddenly, she is goddess again. She no longer laments her function as mother of the dying god. For them, death is not separation, only closeness, union and perpetuity. His essence fuses with hers, spreading from womb to soul.

She uses the knowledge to support her through the ordeal that is still to follow. Attargatis' world stands still. In a daze, she watches Mithras choose a tree and position himself before it. Reverently he accepts the sword from a high priest and holds it high above his naked body. Then, in a single movement he brings it down and severs his testicles. Blood spurts. The priests and priestesses throw back their heads to welcome the ruby splashes. They close their eyes ecstatically and spread out their arms to catch the droplets, then fall to their knees and smear the sacred blood on the grass and the foliage.

Mithras lies down beneath the tree where he will bleed to death. Attargatis looks on. She longs to leave the throne and rush to her beloved, but with an effort she remains where she is. Yet it is only her shell, hovering to deceive all eyes. From within, her essence finds itself beside Mithras. As her tears fall on him, mother-love heals the searing pain in his loins.

He puts his hand to her lips to prevent her speaking. It is strong and vibrant with life. 'Hush. You know I'm with you. And I'll be back in spring, in the flesh. When the hills are honeyed with my new light and the fields are bursting like gold mines, I'll be with you again in body as well.'

At last the song returns to Attagatis' heart. 'And I'll be here.'

Outside dawn is breaking. The priests proclaim that Mithras will return to redeem them and the world. They will await the first signs of his rebirth on the third day of the sacrifice.

Attargatis knows more. Cybele, Astarte, Aphrodite stroke her belly. Inside, Mithras' seed has begun to grow. Nine months from now he will fill the skies with his radiance. The fields will spill forth their bounty. Until then her lover, her son, will live and grow inside her.

Winter at Llanddwyn

The ruined shrine of Dwynwen
patron saint of lovers
Cantref of Rhosyr

*Loss and disillusion turn to forgiveness in this moving
story when a princess torn between her father's will and
her beloved's desire finds liberation in spiritual love.*

Not to dance. To sit it out
In the storm, in the level sunlight
All winter, deciduous.

With wings pegged on the line
Cormorants hang like scarecrows.
The islands are so near.

The gulls' clattering quarrel
Reaches downwind
In a high melancholy wail.

It empties the air,
This winter calm.
There's nothing to think.

Will the prelude
Break on a downbeat,
A crescendo of excitement?

The curtain of time
Stays shut, curls
Only at the edge, like ripples.

Will the cold islands
Reveal themselves
A scena, or *pas de deux*?

A girl here. A man. An expectation.
It was as if in the gentle savagery of love
They danced, hardly touching –

Even a kiss broke the concentration
Of their waiting, even a reaching hand
Startled in a rush of wings.

In the rhyme of bodies, alliterations
Of moving together, mirrorings –
An inseparable separation.

Time was created in the first moments
When their eyes met. Like a dance
In its performance, nothing

Before that counted. Prehistory
Only inferred in the quality
Of gesture, a fossil acquaintance.

But then, she broke it.

– Why?

– There are answers, of course.
Father opposed to it, a dynasty
To be thought of . . . Or was it
A sudden, inexplicable
Failure of belief, an injury
Like a finger cut off
To a fiddler?

– Or did he overreach himself
In some way, and offend her?

– She showed no anger.

– He did, though.

– She had betrayed him?

– Betrayed the two of them. He saw her
Choose to make nothingness
Of what they'd been.
Very well, his body would show her –
Tell her how nothingness felt. He forced her,
Pulled her down, stripped her . . .

– Didn't she cry out?

– He left her, in the contempt he felt for her
A day and a night. She was unclean –
Her father tried to hide her
But there was nowhere left,
Nowhere beyond the mirroring.

– It was terrible for her.

– But he was destroyed by it,
Maddened by the ice
That scooped life out of him
He would have starved . . .

It was then God chose her,
Then, or at the beginning
Of the world, in the nothingness.

It is said that an Angel came
With a new mirroring. He showed her
Maelon, her lover, frozen in the ice.

God gave her three wishes . . .

This winter calm
Empties the air.
There's nothing to think.

Though in the pool
Configurations of fishes
Prophesy (or lovers say they do)

And birds on the islands
Live out their natural
Appetitive hysterias –

The clipped sarcasm of gulls,
The cormorants –
Seals roll on their backs and sing . . .

Yet God chooses
In the nothingness
Before the curtain's drawn

Where the dancers from the green room
Wait to cross into time
As their eyes meet his

And there's nothing to think
But the dance
And the empty light.

I Whirl

Rumi's verses introduced me to eroticism in a most pro-found sense. Striving for union with the True Beloved, sometimes through the aegis of another human being, is the essence of Sufism – a potent love formula. I hope I have conveyed some of its power.

From the shadow of the sun the dew learns of its demise
I, too, exist for the favour of your glance

I didn't write that couplet, it comes from a poet of the future. He must have plucked it from my heart. I think you know that, Shams. My Sun, my blazing, burning Sun. Do you know what it felt like to face, twice in the same lifetime, your sudden, mysterious departure?

– Of course you know.

– You knew my essence and my substance. You knew it more than anyone alive.

– You still went.

I am wandering through the market-place now. Its beloved, familiar alleys. From somewhere in the mêlée comes the clash of metal against metal; an aural symbol flying from the motions of Zarkoob, the goldsmith. People know me here. They point to me or they bow and salute. There is sadness in the eyes of some.

Poor man! they think. He seeks to find the dead.

Others look at me questioningly.

Is this the man who guides us in our quest? they wonder. Is he in the whirlpool of some profound illusion? Some dust-well of the imagination that sucks him under, swivelling and spinning into grainy, fluid darkness that invades every part of his body and soul? Will we benefit from his survival? Will we be enhanced through his experience?

That is the trial of the teacher. That is also his greatest reward.

Clang-clang! Clang! Clang! Few know the significance of Zarkoob's hammer on gold.

In search of you, Shams, I have wandered far and wide. I looked inside strange faces and saw my devastation. I was looking for you but you were not there. What happened to your faith in my conviction that '*no lover seeks unless the beloved desires it*'? What happened to *my* faith? Is it so tied up in you that it seeps like water into sand grains disappearing from the eye in a pulse beat, like you melted into the dark, and I have to ask: 'Do you desire my seeking?'

– I think you must. But still I doubt my thought for so often need becomes the cataract that blurs vision.

– You said once: '*There is something in me which my guide did not see. Nobody ever saw it until my lord, the Mevlevi.*'

– I still see it, Shams, my Sun. I still see that essence.

But where are you?

Like a giant blackbird you swooped into my life then, like a fleet creature, you slipped into the night, your legacy this continuous search. Will the seeking ever stop? Will the journey ever have its end? Or will I be for ever like that sand-writer, that desert-walker, that Great Lover whom they call Majnun, love-crazed? I saw him across time, across space, past fact, past fiction. Do you know his pain?

– You never said you had seen him.

– But you did see the Holy One, God's Prophet, friend of mankind.

– You told me he gave you your mendicant's cloak. It kept you free from cult and caste. You preserved your wild fire, your blazing eyes.

– But I have known the pain of Majnun.

– Shall I tell you about him?

Alone in the waste-land of his desire, that love-crazed desert-wanderer sat writing a letter using his fingers for a pen, the sand for paper. He looked at me, his mind had abandoned his eyes and emptiness glared out.

'I practise the name of Laila, my Beloved,' he cried. 'To ease my own heart, I write.'

Shall I sacrifice myself for you, as he did for her? I'll tell you the end of Majnun, the love-crazed, of Farhad, the Mountain-pounder, of all the great lovers and their friend. Do you know how they were united, Shams?

They were united in death. While housed in the body, the soul may simply sense the soul of the Beloved Other. Through the body we can breathe its sacred scent, we can glimpse its veiled light, we can hear its magic music. We can guess what it will be to touch and merge – we do not experience the touching and merging. The body is clay – set in its shape and its integrity.

The soul? It is fire. It leaps and dances, stretches and shrinks – sways and sends out sparks.

The epiphany, Shams? What is the epiphany? A veil, a burst of light, a gust of music – signs that say it is elsewhere.

Clang-clang! Clang! Clang! Clang-clang! Clang! Clang!

Zarkoob's hammer pounds gold. Now it seems to resonate with my heart, that clanging.

Long-short/long-long/long-short/long-long/long-short/long-long/Long-short-long.

Ah! I see it now. His hammer strokes reflect my poetry's rhythms. My favourite prosody. Ramal – sand, they call it, because it slips water-like through the fingers. There it is again! I hear it name the prosody now. Masterly, full of the knowledge of the rhythm in my veins.

Fa-i-la-tun/fa-i-la-tun/fa-i-la-tun/fa-i-lun.

Those syllables are the rhythm, the meter, the grammar of love. Their feet will walk through my life's vast desert, the blooming wilderness of my love, their vibrations set adrift the clouds through which Shams will shine again. They will illuminate my discourse. They will give voice to my passion. They will light the fires of my desire. Fa-i-la-tun . . .

Fa-i-la-tun . . . my desires. I remember those heady days when we sat in Zarkoob's cell. The world saw us talk, heard our discourse. But how much more we did! We touched the skies with the tips of our tongues, we glanced at heaven, we warmed in the glow of divine fires. I recall that first meeting.

'Which meeting?' Salahudin Zarkoob's voice asks me.

'Have I come to the goldsmith already?' I ask, surprised. 'And am I thinking aloud?'

Zarkoob's eyes shine with a fine glaze of tears. He is saddened by my love-lunacy.

'There is nothing to be sad for, my friend,' I reassure him. 'It is just love. We rejoice in love.'

People look down on my friend Zarkoob. They think him an illiterate artisan. But Zarkoob has an enlightened soul. A soul of gold. He and I learned side by side from the same great Master. I saw his soul transmuted in God's alchemical vessel. But Zarkoob's heartbeats still say 'I'. He has not yet found 'We'.

'Are you recalling the memory of your first meeting?' he asks.

'A caravanserai. He was hiding but I knew I had to find him.'

You told me how you had passed all three stages of love to become the Axis of All Beloved. Yet you never found the love you sought. And you asked God.

'Is there no one among your élite who can bear my companionship?'

'Go to Rumi,' His voice told you.

If our first meeting was night then the second was day, as vivid to me as my reflection in the cool, distant water of the fountain. I sat bathed in the gentle sun of late October. It embraced my skin, clinging like a blanket still warm from the imprint of the love-play of mother and infant. I pored through books in my constant pursuit of wisdom. I sought the truth. I searched for answers. Yes, in those days I still searched for answers in books. But you arrived and taught me to search first for the questions.

You invaded my thoughts like a life-claiming bird of prey. Your eyes flashed, your hair flew around you, your cloaked

arms spread like a great black bird as you seized my books,
my only treasure, and hurled them into the water. I watched,
devastated.

'Why don't you speak?' you demanded. 'Don't you know
the words of the question?'

I shook my head mutely. I saw the dissolution of the ink of
years of striving. I saw the wisdom of Ibn Arabi drowning. I
watched divine knowledge washed away. Tears filled my
eyes. The sun in the sky had lost its warmth.

'You weep over pieces of paper?' you demanded. 'If that is
what you want, have them back.'

You lifted out one of those books. It was undamaged and
dry. I looked at it and saw for the first time. The words were
intact but they were no longer anything more than ink
scratches.

'Leave them there,' I replied. 'Water is a good resting
place.'

You smiled, sun-warmth caressed and embraced me. This
time it infiltrated my soul. I was lit up from inside. Suddenly
I remembered the meaning of your name. Shams – the Sun.
Strange, isn't it, how we rarely associate meaning with the
names that label people?

There was so much to say. So much to discuss that was
not yet written. So many questions to formulate in service of
the soul. You lent us your cell, Zarkoob. And it was as if we
stayed there, discoursing for six months.

You, Shams, were wild – to preserve your strong spirit, I
think. You had travelled many nations, sought out many
scholars but were impressed with none. You made me laugh
with your cursory dismissal of minds generally deemed great.
You said:

'Did I tell you about my meeting with the Master from Kerman? The one they say can see the true beauty of all created things? He was looking into a bowl of water by the window of his room. As I entered, he turned and looked at me, sighing.

'"I have just seen the moon reflected in this bowl of water," he said. "What beauty!"

'"Have you got a boil on your neck?" I wanted to know. He shook his head. "Then why not look at the sky?"'

'"But you, Jelaleddin of Rum, are a master of masters,"' you said. '"You have chosen to look at the moon in the sky, in its freedom and splendour and infinity – not its reflection confined in a clay vessel. If Ibn Arabi is a pebble on the shores of infinity, you are a pearl."'

People began to stare at us. Looks turned to whispers, whispers to calumny. The susurration of calumny is loud and cuts deep. Shams lost patience with it. One day he disappeared.

'You do not know what you have done,' I told them.

'You did nothing but talk to that man,' they complained. 'You stopped teaching us. You neglected classes. You paid no attention to our needs.'

'It is all part of the process of learning,' I replied. 'Did it never occur to you that a teacher is only human? He can't teach without the benefit of learning. He must nurture his mind and his soul. He must probe the secrets of the spirit, attempt to grasp the veil of the Hidden One. You have harmed me. You have invaded the realm of my inspiration, you have ambushed me on my journey to knowledge. Now I must leave you to continue my search elsewhere. I must find Shams and bring him back.'

That was when I left, wandering far and wide.

It was a great day when you returned from Damascus on the arm of my son and successor Sultan Valad. To ensure you would stay, I married you to Kimiya, who had grown up in my household after her parents died. We spent many ecstatic years together, exploring the depths of the eternal. Through our respective families, the pleasure and pain of the phenomenological world enriched us. Together we exchanged the courage to grasp the infinite. To discourse with the unseen. If I spoke of the *sirr-e-nihaan*, the Hidden Secret, then you asked me: 'What is the significance of the hidden? Can that which is already secret be hidden as well?' I laughed. You always directed me to the question that would unlock the answer. The quest for the Hidden Secret was nothing if I did not know the question. How many layers and worlds of knowledge that question revealed! What complexities in the dissection of the simplest phrase! But journeys do not continue uninterrupted. Even when you seek the question with the greatest sincerity, event is concentration's enemy.

– Why were you distracted in the deep of that night?

– Why did you answer that call from the darkness? Why did you not continue speaking as you had so many times before, ignoring the outside world?

'No one denies the call of Azrafeel.' Zarkoob's voice was so soft, I heard it with my intuition.

'Azrafeel?'

'They say he was murdered that night. Murdered and thrown into a well. Later they dragged his body from the well and buried it in a grave sealed with plaster. They covered over the grave with mud and trees and grass. It looked part of the wilderness. Azrafeel, Angel of Death, visited that night, with those other killers.

'So Shams is dead? The Sun is dead. Will there be light again?' I thought of the devastation of the world without the Sun. I felt breathless. The power left my limbs as I ingested the hideous truth.

'Truth? Do you give the name of Truth to a phenomenon, an inevitable, banal event?'

The voice thundered from within and I shook with the power of its vibrations.

Clang-clang! Clang! Clang! Zarkoob has picked up his hammer.

I searched for you and could not find you. You do not find the Friend in the firmament or the soil. You find him in your heart. From my mind welled up the completions to all those fragmentary thoughts of the past. The questions I had forgotten to find before I found Shams in that crazed frenetic search. Had I ever asked, 'Where is Shams?' Had I ever thought, If no lover searches unless the beloved desires it, then why is Shams not searching for me? I see now, that I doubted your love. I doubted your commitment without even knowing. I became so conscious of this world of phenomena, so aware of my body and its pain, I forgot the sensations of the soul.

– I did not know you no longer needed to seek me.

– That you had abandoned 'I and you' to become 'we'.

– But now?

– But now you have transformed. I celebrate your liberation. I drink again of our divine wine.

I begin to swell. The shell that is my body fills with sensuous warmth infusing my heart and my belly, flooding my limbs. The warmth lights a spark that floats, drunken, upwards. My head explodes with unspoken ecstasy. The joy of union. The joy of never parting again. The joy of being We.

Slowly, I start to turn. One wrist twists, its palm turns to the ground like an upturned goblet. I raise my right arm, cup the palm to the sky. My body is the stem connecting my palms, the bowls of the flower-cup of Being. I receive from the sky, bestow on the earth. I keep turning. My movements continue. From sky to earth; from sky to earth. From sky to earth, the sands of divinity, of time, of space, begin to flow.

My eyes are shut against the external world. My face turns upwards. I feel the breezes of my own making beginning to stir and caress my cheeks, warm from the spark stoked within me to a flame which will one day consume me entirely.

Ecstasy! You are the mirage in my revolving eye – the true reality beyond this strange illusion we call the world of phenomena.

I sense Zarkoob rising, beginning to turn. Whirling.

'I whirl, Mevlevi,' he cries out. 'I whirl with you. Tell me what makes you whirl? Is it the memory of Shams, that wild black bird?'

Laughter bubbles up like lava from the ground of my being and erupts through me. Memory? We do not need memories of constant companions.

And so it is, I come to whirl.

– You are in the strains of my music,

– You are in the thoughts of my song.

– You are the stir of air my dancing causes.

– You are both the stillness and the fire within me.

– I have experienced you.

My eyes fall on Zarkoob's paraphernalia. I know now you have burned away the dross and transmuted into pure gold.

Notes

SECTION ONE: **Awakenings**

The City of Longing

Aamer Hussein reworked this story from the celebrated Persian *Haft Paikar* (Seven Visages/Beauties) by Nizami Ganjevi of Ganja near Azarbaijan in Iran. Nizami was known for his *khamsa*, quintet, which include the renowned love tragedies *Shirin Farhad* and *Laila Majnun* both well known throughout the Islamic world.

Aamer wrote the story especially for this volume. His knowledge of Persian and Urdu texts is awesome and his two highly praised collections of short stories, *Mirror to the Sun* (Mantra, 1993) and *This Other Salt* (Saqi, 1999) both include tales inspired by fairytales from the Islamic cultural regions. Also his work tackles notably a range of erotic attitudes.

A Pastoral Song

The story of Radha and Krishna is best known from the erotic Indian poem 'Geeta Govinda' (The Song of Govinda) by Jayadeva (twelfth or thirteenth century). Set in the district of Mathura, the text focuses on the pastoral god Krishna (also known as Govinda, the cowherd) and his romantic games with the *gopis*, or milkmaids. His erotic activities, mostly played out in the forest of Vrindavan (also pronounced Brindaban), symbolize the human soul's quest to merge with divinity. Radha personifies the soul entrapped in human form with all its demands, social, physical and material. The journey to the Beloved is beset with hardships and sacrifice and fuelled only by the yearning that follows the first spark of spiritual recognition, a vision of union, which becomes obsessive and undeniable. Several translations exist of 'Geeta Govinda', most of them poor. Another text comparable in content appeared in the fourteenth century composed by Vidhyapati, a poet writing in Maithili and celebrated as one of the greatest poets of Krishna verse. This was the text I used, from the shelves at home. It is translated by Dr Subhadra Jha, under the title *The Songs of Vidhyapati* (Motilal Banarsidass, Banaras, India, 1954).

The images and erotic elements in my retelling are close to the evocative Indian original. The themes of 'Geeta Govinda' are found frequently in the lyrics of the vocal classical music of India as well as in popular hymns.

Amaltheia and Chryse

From *The Affairs of Zeus* by Harry Robin, 1st Books, the International Online Library, US, 1996. Written from the viewpoint of Zeus looking back after the Olympian era is

over, this book 'recounts his love affairs with several goddesses, nymphs and mortal women'. Sexual intercourse
remained Zeus' favourite pastime, despite the castigations of
his sister-wife Hera, patron of marriage and fidelity, for his
many betrayals. Zeus is known to be rapacious and indis-
criminate in sexual pursuit but Robin has brought
tenderness and freshness to his tales – Zeus as the young
innocent, eager and prodigious in the hands of a highly experienced female.

The Vernal Palace

From *The Carnal Prayermat* by Li Yu (tr. unknown),
Wordsworth Classics (Classical Erotica series), pp. 21–41.
Lady Noble Scent is the stuff of potent, erotic fantasies: a
repressed virgin waiting for her raging sexuality to be unbri-
dled. The story introduces the reader to the medieval
Chinese techniques of love. Its author Li Yu (b. 1610) was a
prolific writer and the director of a travelling theatre. This
novel, full of fun and surprises, is set between 1280 and 1368
during the reign of the Mongol dynasty, and tells of a travelling Buddhist student's dedication to eroticism. It was first
published in 1634. The extract reproduced here consists of
most of Chapter II. The chapters are untitled: I took the
name from the sex manual central to the story.

The Arousal of Inanna

This Sumerian goddess is cognate with Ishtar, of Akkadian
myth. Hymns were sung to her from around 3000 BCE. The
systematic excavation of the tablets recording the sophisti-
cated civilizations of Sumer began as late as 1842 and the
cuneiform code on the tablets and cylinders was not sub-

stantially interpreted until 1905. In the mid-twentieth century significant archaeological discoveries continued to be
made and Samuel Noah Kramer, perhaps the best known of
the Sumeriologists, 'discovered' the myth of Inanna's journey
to the Underworld, in the sixties.

The Inanna of the poems here is a gentle maiden, a fertility goddess, whose body responds to the pleasures of nascent
sexual desire. The Sumerian verses have been much translated, the best-known version being *Inanna, Queen of Heaven
and Earth, Her Stories and Hymns from Sumer*, Harper & Row,
NY, 1983. Folklorist and storyteller Diana Wolkstein translated it in collaboration with Kramer and took it to a wide,
non-academic audience, which made Inanna something of an
icon and a psychological archetype for women in the United
States and Britain (see also *Descent to the Goddess, A Way of
Initiation for Women*, by Jungian analyst Sylvia Brinton
Perera. Inner City Books, Canada, 1981). Wolkstein and
Kramer's book is perhaps the most celebrated account of the
goddess where she visits the Great Above to be consecrated
as goddess and then the Great Below to gain a victory over
the Underworld. On her visit to her grandfather in the skies,
she receives untold gifts. Ranking equally with life and death
are the *'art of lovemaking!'* and *'the kissing of the phallus'*
(Wolkstein and Kramer, p. 15) – a testament to the value the
Sumerians placed on sexual proficiency.

For the selection of songs and verses here, telling the
story of Inanna's sexual awakening and initiation, I scoured
many translations, until I found Yitschak Sefati's *Love Songs
in Sumeria, A Critical edition of the Dumuzi-Inanna Songs*, (Bar-
llan University Press, Israel, 1998). The author had
arranged the pieces in a cycle so that together they form a

satisfying account which is essentially story-shaped. I have substantially rewritten and rearranged the material drawn from various translations. Sumerian verse is rhythmically repetitive, in common with the religious verse of many languages; in English, its prosody is unfamiliar. Its language, primarily translated for an academic audience concerned with authentic replication, is archaic, often containing images so alien that they can be bizarre or ludicrous. I felt it impossible to tinker with a few lines and phrases because they feel perfect as translated: for example when Inanna refers to her bridegroom's 'honey sweetness'. References to the bull, scattered throughout the poem, are also left unchanged since the imagery of the hero-lover and the bull are integral to the geographical area particularly in the widespread sun-hero/sacral kingship myths. Gilgamesh, Enkidu, Mithras and Adonis have all been compared to the bull, probably to convey their power generally but also with regard to their genitalia. In an agrarian culture, a bull is infinitely more relevant than another animal symbolizing potent sexuality, such as a stallion might be today.

My main debt of gratitude goes to Yitschak Sefati: I used his work as the main inspiration for my rewrite and his phrases are scattered throughout the piece.

SECTION TWO: Desire

The Tobacco Plant

From *North American Indian Mythology* by Cotti Burland, Paul Hamlyn, London, 1965. Part of the mythology of the southern tribes of North America, this little story provides an understanding of the significance of tobacco in the world of the American Indian tribes. In another tale tobacco originated from the bones of the Corn Mother or First Woman, after she had sacrificed her life to provide food for her family. The tobacco leaf provided a source of relaxation and peace-making. The point here is that much of what gives pleasure and eases relations in the world comes in some way from true love and union. These stories survived orally, often in fragments, but I wonder if they were at some time more explicit in the hands of the story-tellers who, no doubt, told them in many versions over the centuries. Too often, when the tales came to be written they were bowdlerized in the interest of appeasing contemporaneous morality and the originals were eventually lost and forgotten.

Izanagi and Izanami

This is one of the best-known myths of the Japanese pantheon in the western world, even though it is somewhat overshadowed by the story of their daughter, Amaterasu, sun goddess, who is still worshipped in Japan. The other well-known story about Izanami and Izanagi belongs to the Orpheus and Eurydice tradition where a grieving husband attempts to deliver his wife from the Underworld. It completes the introduction to Japanese eschatology begun in the myth here about the heavenly and earthly realms, with its depiction of the Underworld as a phase in the lifecycle.

My source for this retelling were the *Kojiki* and the *Nihongi* in translation. I used elements from both of the above texts, which provide literally dozens of versions of this short 'record', highlighting minuscule textual differences. I have merged the few variant elements from different accounts to make this retelling as full as possible. These include, significantly, the return of the primal couple of Japan to heaven to ensure that their interaction is begun with suitable regard to custom and also the instruction on copulation from the water birds. W.J. Aston (George Allen and Unwin Ltd, 1956), bursts into Latin at this point – a wonderful piece of literary coyness and a common censorship device. I have tried to reproduce the factual, unembellished style of the original narratives, hence the brevity of the piece. The *Kojiki* is a compilation based on a lost 'history of the Emperors of Japan and of matters of high antiquity' commissioned in 682 CE. The *Nihongi*, also a compilation, was presented at court in 720 CE.

The Queen of the Summer Country

The Queen of the Summer Country by Rosalind Miles, Simon and Schuster, London, 1999, pp. 500–510. The episode at Dolorous Garde follows the abduction of Guenevere by her kinsman, the Knight Malgaunt. It is the traditional rape of the Flower Maiden from pagan Britain but also mirrors Pluto's abduction of Persephone in Hellenic myth. Blathnat and Curoi from Ireland fit into the same mould – Blathnat (Flower Woman) is abducted by Curoi and rescued by Cu Chullin. Guenevere herself represents spring and spring flowers, and her rescuer is the chivalrous Lancelot. Birth, growth and reproduction are an important element of spring so monogamy in a spring goddess would be counter-productive. Another Flower Maiden is Blodeuwedd from Welsh myth, who betrayed her husband Llewu Llaw Gyffes for a hunter. Malgaunt represents the Wild Man of the

Woods, a lascivious fertility god like Pan, also cognate with the preservation of the wilderness.

The love of Guenevere and Lancelot also falls into another category of stories common to British myth and legend featuring a leader who is displaced in the affections of his wife or his betrothed, by a much-favoured younger follower. Examples include Grainne and Diarmuid, Deirdre and Naoise and, perhaps most famously, Tristan and Isolde. In the hands of the troubadours, such stories became popular as examples of a love so profound and impossible it could only be realized in death. As such it fell into the category of 'distant' love and became comparable to a mystic's devotion to God.

Eset's Love Quest

This retelling is based on the well-known Heliopolis myth of the Egyptian goddess Isis' search for her twin-lover Osiris. Her ancient name was Eset or Au-set. The Greeks invented the synthetic 'Isis' much later in order to merge her with female divinities from their own pantheon. I was much inspired by some ancient love songs included in the three volumes of *Ancient Egyptian Literature* by Miriam Lichteheim (University of California Press, 1980). The incantation in Isis' last dream of Osiris came from there and elements from others appear elsewhere in the story: Osiris' incantation on his way to the gods; Eset's barring of the doors; when Isis arrives to heal Osiris. The atmosphere of the pieces is very close to the Song of Songs, combining descriptions of the beloved and the passionate yearning that simmers in that famous and fabulous biblical chapter. I wonder if they had a common source.

The motif of the goddess searching for a loved one recurs over and over again in mythologies around the world from perhaps the best-known Greek variant featuring Demeter. Others tell of Pele, the Hawaiian volcano goddess, and the Icelandic Freya. Also Izanami and Izanagi and Orpheus and Eurydice where the lost partner is a female (see page 282). Essentially it is part of a complex of myths symbolizing the seasonal cycle. The desolation of the earth, the withering and disappearance of vegetation is a metaphor for autumn and winter, the third of the year when Persephone *et al.* remained in the Underworld. The return represents spring and regeneration. (See also 'The Sacrifice', page 292.)

The Ballad of Skirnir

This poem is part of the Poetic Edda of Iceland by Snorri Sturluson dated between 1177 and 1350. I worked from an edition printed by the American-Scandinavian Foundation: *The Poetic Edda* by Henry Adams Bellows, 1923. I modernized the language but preserved the four-line verse structure. Occasionally, I introduced an explanatory phrase, for example that Odin's son was Baldur, or that the names of the giants linked them to the frost. Gerth, the heroine's name, means 'field of barley' and Skirnir is the 'Shining One', pointing to the seasonal tussle of winter (Gerth's frosty kin) with spring, or summer. This is seen everywhere in myth – for example, 'Caellie Bheur of Scotland' (*The Virago Book of Witches*, p. 213 and note 5, p. 242). Other examples include the struggle between St Columcill and the Lord of the Underworld at Glastonbury Tor.

SECTION THREE: **Games of Love**

Maui

From *God – Myths of the Male Divinity*, David Leeming and Jake Page (pp. 25–7). This story, from the islands of the South Pacific, tells of a goddess in search of sexual pleasure. Maui, the famed trickster and culture hero of the area, once attempted to be reborn by entering the womb of his grand-mother, the Great Goddess Hine, through her vagina – Freud would have enjoyed the Oedipal connotations. In other versions Maui is the son of Taranga, who threw him into the sea because he was not properly formed at birth. (There are echoes here of the Vedic Martand, dead egg, laid by Aditi. Martand survived to become Surya, the Sun, in Hindu myth.) Later, when Maui was introduced, fully devel-oped, to her, Taranga showered him with honours. He was also a wanderer and a trickster and is sometimes called the Polynesian Ulysses.

Hera's Deceit

The account of this interaction between Hera and Zeus is based closely on the sequence of episodes in Homer's *Iliad*. The description at the end, of the *hieros gamos*, the traditional coming together or sacred marriage of Zeus and Hera, is my reworking of a widely quoted passage. I'm not sure where the translation originated.

The Conception of Hatshepsut

This story is based on the paintings in the temple of Hatshepsut at Deir el-Bari near Luxor in the Valley of the Kings after the queen-pharaoh had invented the episode to validate her claim to the throne. Hatshepsut (1504–1482 BCE) had the distinction of being the first significant woman pharaoh. The pharaoh was thought to represent Amun-Re on earth and was therefore male. Thutmose I, Hatshepsut's father, groomed her for rulership and after his death she married her half-brother, Thutmose II, who died in 1479 BCE, leaving her as regent to his underage son Thutmose III. In 1472 she declared herself pharaoh and began a reign distinguished by huge achievements in the fields of commerce, architecture, industry and politics. She disappeared mysteriously in 1458 BCE when Thutmose III regained his position as pharaoh. Thutmose appears to have made every possible effort to wipe all trace of his rival. Her mummy was never found. Her name means 'The Noble Best'

El

From *Mythologies of the Ancient World*, translated by Cyrus H. Gordon, edited and introduced by Samuel Noah Kramer, Anchor, Doubleday, 1961 (pp. 186–90). The extract here comes from the chapter on Canaanite mythology. It forms part of a larger piece, originally a ritual drama in ancient Ugaritic, performed every seven years. El, an aged god, creates the two women, shoots a bird and kills it, then approaches the women, penis (rod) lowered. Incredibly, his success or failure in winning the women was unscripted; yet on it depended the well-being of the next years of the nation. Acceptance of El's phallus indicated successful fertilization of the fields but rejection meant the land would suffer drought. What a burden for the performers!

Aroma's Trick

From *The Carnal Prayermat* by Li Yu (tr. unknown), Wordsworth Classics (Classical Erotica series), pp. 133–45. Li Yu was obviously playing to many audiences when he made his sly assessment of the shenanigans around him. Miss Aroma's waggish plot provides a vehicle for the writer to take an amicable pop at the outrageousness of women on their own, especially in regard to the sex games they play, men's superficiality in being attracted only to a beautiful face, and the importance of preserving the masculine myth of 'staying power' in bed. The beauty is that even while it challenges prevailing attitudes, this bawdy adventure allows everyone to triumph in the end.

SECTION FOUR: **Tales of Lust and Ribaldry**

The Lusty Lass

From *Medieval Welsh Erotic Poetry* (*Canu Maswedd yr Oesoedd Canol*), edited and translated by Dafydd Johnstone, Seren, Wales, 1998, pp. 77–9. The strong, rural imagery of this poem, written in the medieval period, is reminiscent of some of the beliefs of the old pre-Christian religions. The country lass pleads openly to be 'ploughed' echoing the discourse of a Mother Goddess culture in which woman symbolizes the fields. The woman's bold invitations and the boy's fearful responses suggest a power dynamic we don't generally relate to that period. On the other hand, the insatiable temptress is part of classic male fantasy.

Dahama and Moussa

From *The Perfumed Garden, A Manual of Arabian Erotology*, translated by Sir Richard Burton, privately published by the Kama Shastra Society, 1886. These stories are from Nafzawi's book (see note below, 'The Man of Quality'). Burton's two other comparable works, *Kama Sutra* and *Ananga-ranga*, were translated from Indian erotica. So far, only selections of Nafzawi's work have been translated for a western audience. Burton is said to have completed a further thousand pages of a section on homosexuality and pederasty the day before he died on 19 October 1890. His wife Isabel found the work and burnt it. In fact, all his work had been strictly censored by his wife, or for her benefit, since their meeting in 1850.

Daghda

This retelling is based on an extract from *Cath Maige Tuired* (pronounced Moy Tirra), *The Second Battle of Mag Tuired*, edited by Elizabeth A. Gray and published by the Irish Texts Society, 1982. I first came across the account in Dr Daithi O Hogain's magnificent book *Myth, Legend and Romance, An Encyclopaedia of Irish Folk Tradition,* Prentice Hall Press, 1991, p. 145. Dr O Hogain very kindly provided me with this translation from the Irish.

In the mythological cycle of Ireland, the Daghda was the father-god of the Tuatha de Danaan, the fairy folk who took over Ireland after winning the two battles of Maige Tuired against the monstrous occupants called the Fomoire. Morrigan is here because of her significant role in battle as a war goddess. The promiscuity of Daghda, which means Father, is part of his function as a fertility god. Dr O Hogain points out that this account, like many other myths and legends of Ireland, was recorded by Christian missionaries who found the old gods contemptible and sought to discredit them as grotesque and reprehensible.

The Man of Quality

From *The Perfumed Garden of Sensual Delight* translated by Jim Colville, Kegan Paul International, London, 1999, pp. 6–10 and pp. 10–17. The original in Arabic came from the pen of a Tunisian scholar, Umar Ibn Muhammad Al-Nafzawi, around 1510. Written at the height of the Tunisian empire when the capital was unrestrainedly opulent and dynamic, it is a humorous and bawdy work, which is sometimes compared to Boccaccio. Modern translations reflect its sexual directness and detail far more than Burton's much earlier and less authentic efforts (see 'Dahama and Moussa', note above). It has never been translated in full.

SECTION FIVE: Love Beyond Life (or The Rapturous Gaze)

Powder Figures

This interlude is part of one of the core incidents of the Indian epic *Mahabharata*, recorded *c.* 2000 BCE. Bhishma, born of the king's marriage to the goddess Ganga, the river Ganges incarnate, is the driving and unifying force of much of the epic. It fell to him to find a wife for his half-brother Vichitra Virya born of Queen Satyavati, who had been a fisherwoman. He abducted the three princesses, Amba, Ambika and Ambalika. When he discovered that Amba was already engaged, he returned her to her betrothed. But the king rejected her and she swore vengeance. She returned, decades later, incarnated as a male warrior. It was she who struck the blow that eventually killed the invincible Bhishma.

The two remaining sisters married King Vichitra Virya, son of Santanu and Satyavati. Ananda Devi takes up the story here and brings to life the bizarre pact between the mother-in-law and the young queens to give the kingdom an heir.

Rishi Vyasa was also the son of the 'old queen' Satyavati, through congress with a *rishi* (sage). Ambika's blind son was Dhritarashtra, who fathered the hundred Kauravas, and Ambalika bore Pandu from whom the five Pandavas took their names (although, in fact they were fathered by various gods). I am grateful to Ananda Devi for writing this piece so swiftly in response to my request for a contribution. Ananda Devi is from Mauritius and generally writes in French. Among her various novels is one based on Dhraupadi, the magnificent polyandrous female from the *Mahabharata*, *The Veil of Dhraupadi*, *Le Voile de Draupadi*, Éditions L'Harmatton, 1993. Her latest novel *Pagli*, is published by Gallimard.

Sappho

Sappho's Lyre, Archaic Lyric and Women Poets of Ancient Greece, translated by Diane J. Rayor, University of California Press, 1991. Sappho was writing in the late seventh century. Most of her work, much admired in her time, is lost to us. The poem here, in which she appeals to Aphrodite to bring her love to her, is the only complete survival. She lived and worked in Mytilene on Lesbos. Scholars believe that sexual love between women may have been considered normal before marriage in Sappho's time.

The Sacrifice

The goddess of this story is Attargatis whose son-lover was Mithras. Also known as Dea Syria, this goddess is cognate with others from around the general region of ancient Anatolia, Babylon and Mesopotamia where myths of the mother-son dyad were common. In this story type, an older goddess such as Cybele, fell in love with a younger man such as Attis. The most famous such myth is of Venus/Aphrodite and Adonis, who represents her son. The myth is bound up with parthenogenesis, belief in the rebirth of the sun, sacral kingship and the regeneration of crops. Theoretically, the Great Goddess is the mother of every existing creature and therefore every male is her son. In ancient Egypt the pharaoh, who was god incarnate, was required to be ritually sacrificed, usually in a bloody manner, so that his blood replenished the soil. His person represented the land, and the ageing process accompanied by illness, weakness and general decay projected its negativities into the earth. In practice, the king often found some hapless surrogate, who was fed and venerated as king for a time before being killed in his place. Echoes of the customs of sacral kingship are present as far afield as Ireland and certainly all over the Near Eastern regions of Israel, Sumeria and Anatolia where this myth originated.

The sacrificial rite that followed the marriage of the goddess to her son bears a great many similarities to the story of Christ: death from slow bleeding at the height of youth, the return on the third day for the redemption/continuation of the world. Note also similarities with Baldur in Scandinavian myth and Lleu Llaw Gyffes in Welsh myth, both associated with light and sun and sometimes termed myths of the 'bleeding god', the 'suspended god' and the 'returning god/hero'. The priests of Cybele entrusted with re-enacting the tableau of the marriage of the divine couple and the subsequent sacrifice, were known to become impassioned and castrate themselves in dedication to the goddess. I tried, while retelling, to imagine the ambivalence of a woman veering between maternal feelings, sexual desire and that certain objectivity associated with divinity.

Winter at Llanddwyn

By Tony Conran, in *An Anglesey Anthology*, edited by Dewi Matthews, Gwasg Carreg Gwalch, Wales 1999, pp. 64–8. The poem subsequently appeared in Tony Conran's own selection, *A Gwynedd Symphony*, Gomer Press, Ceredigion, 1999. Dwynwen was a Welsh princess who lived in the fifth century. The story goes that she was obliged by her father to end her relationship with her lover, a local chieftain Maelon, for a more appropriate match arranged by her father, the king. Distraught by rejection, Maelon raped her and was turned to ice. Dwynwen became a nun and God granted her three wishes. She asked for her lover to be released from his frozen state, for her prayers on behalf of other lovers to be answered, and never again to fall in love. Traditions of Dwynwen abound in North Wales where she is known as the Welsh Aphrodite and the patron saint of lovers.

I Whirl

Jelaleddin Rumi is best known in the west for founding the mystic (Sufi) order of the whirling dervishes. He was an ecstatic from Konya, Turkey, where his family fled from the Mongol invasions between 1215 and 1220 and headed a school of Sufi mysticism established by his father. His two major works were the *Mathnawi Maulana Rum* (Couplets of the Mevlevi of Rum) and the *Diwan of Shemsuddin Tabrizi*, lyrical poems dedicated to his companion and mentor. His work has been extensively translated into English and he has been voted one of the most popular poets in America. The freely translated works of Coleman Barks are among the best.

Acknowledgements

The publishers gratefully acknowledge the following for permission to reprint copyright material:

Extract from *The Perfumed Garden* copyright© Jim Colville (trs) 1999, reprinted by permission of Kegan Paul International. *Winter at Llanddwyn* copyright © Tony Conran 1999, published by Gomer Press. Extract from *Mythologies of the Ancient World* copyright © Samuel N. Kramer (ed) 1961, reprinted by permission of Doubleday, a division of Random House, Inc. Extract from *God: Myths of thr Male Divine* copyright © Dacid Leeming and Jake Page, reprinted by permission of Oxford University Press, Inc. Extract from *Guenevere: The Queen of the Summer Country* copyright © Rosalind Miles 1999, reprinted with permission of Simon & Schuster. Extract from *Sappho's Lyre: Archaic Lyric and Women Poets of Ancient Greece* copyright © Diane Rayor 1991, reprinted by permission of University of California Press. Extract from *The Affairs of Zeus* copyright © Harry Robin 1996, published by International Online Library, US.

Every effort has been made to trace original copyright holders in all the copyright material included in this book and to provide the correct details of copyright. Virago regret any oversight and upon written notification will rectify any omission in future reprints or editions.